Series/Number 07-133

D0162168

TRANSLATING QUESTIONNAIRES AND OTHER RESEARCH INSTRUMENTS: PROBLEMS AND SOLUTIONS

ORLANDO BEHLING
Behling Associates

KENNETH S. LAW
Hong Kong University of Science and Technology

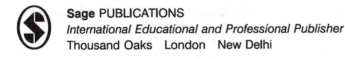

Sage PUBLICATIONS
International Educational and Professional Publisher
Thousand Oaks London New Delhi

For information:

Sage Publications, Inc.
2455 Teller Road
Thousand Oaks, California 91320
E-mail: order@sagepub.com

Sage Publications Ltd.
6 Bonhill Street
London EC2A 4PU
United Kingdom

Sage Publications India Pvt. Ltd.
M-32 Market
Greater Kailash I
New Delhi 110 048 India

Printed in the United States of America

Library of Congress Cataloging-in-Publication Data

Behling, Orlando.
    Translating questionnaires and other research instruments: Problems and solutions / Orlando Behling, Kenneth S. Law.
    p.   cm. — (Quantitative applications in the social sciences; no. 07-133)
Includes bibliographical references.
    ISBN 0-7619-1824-8 (acid-free paper)
    1. Questionnaires — Translating.   2. Social surveys — Translating.
I. Law, Kenneth S. II. Title. III. Sage university papers series.
Quantitative applications in the social sciences; no. 07-133.
    HM537.B44 2000
    300'.7'23–dc21   00-008368

This book is printed on acid-free paper.

    01   02   03   04   05   06   7   6   5   4   3   2

Acquiring Editor:	C. Deborah Laughton
Editorial Assistant:	Eileen Carr
Production Editor:	Diana E. Axelsen
Production Assistant:	Cindy Bear
Typesetter:	Technical Typesetting Inc.

When citing a university paper, please use the proper form. Remember to cite the Sage University Paper series title and include paper number. One of the following formats can be adapted (depending on the style manual used):

(1) Behling and Law (2000) *Translating Questionnaires and Other Research Instruments: Problems and Solutions.* Sage University Papers Series on Quantitative Applications in the Social Sciences, 07-131. Thousand Oaks, CA: Sage.

OR

(2) Behling and Law (2000). *Translating Questionnaires and Other Research Instruments: Problems and Solutions* (Sage University Papers Series on Quantitative Applications in the Social Sciences, series no. 07-131). Thousand Oaks, CA: Sage.

CONTENTS

Series Editor's Introduction   v

Acknowledgment   vii

1. An Overview   1
   Two Critical Questions   2
      Should We Translate Questionnaires?   2
      Can We Translate Questionnaires?   4
   The Bottom Line   6

2. Characteristics of Useful Measures   9
   Basic Requirements   9
      Reliability   10
      Validity   11
      Utility   14
      Legality   15
   Equivalence   15
      Semantic Equivalence   15
      Conceptual Equivalence   16
      Normative Equivalence   16

3. Solving Semantic Problems   16
   The Nature of Semantic Problems   16
   Solving Semantic Problems When Translating an
      Existing Instrument   17
      Simple Direct Translation   18
      Modified Direct Translation   19
      Translation/Back-Translation   19
      Ultimate Test   22
      Parallel Blind Technique   23
      Random Probe Technique   23
   Solving Semantic Problems When Creating a
      New Instrument   24
      Write With Translation in Mind   24

      Three Approaches to Solving Semantic Problems When
         Creating a New Instrument 28

4. Solving Conceptual Problems **31**
    Logical Tests of Conceptual Equivalence 32
    Empirical Tests of Conceptual Equivalence 33
       Tests of the Similarity of Factorial Structures 33
       Tests of the Similarity of Positions in
         Nomological Nets 36
       Tests of the Similarity of Scores 36

5. Solving Normative Problems **41**
    Kinds of Normative Problems 42
       Openness With Which Topics Are Discussed 42
       Manner in Which Ideas Are Expressed 43
       Ways in Which Strangers Are Treated 45
    Solutions to Normative Problems 46
       Develop Close Relations With Respondents or Use
         Trusted Agents 47
       Provide Assurances of Anonymity or Confidentiality 47
       Rethink the Translator's Role 48
       Use Decentering or Multicultural Teams 48
       Pilot Test and Field Test 49
       Check Statistically 49

6. Putting It All Together **51**
    What We Did in the Preceding Chapters 51
    What We Do in This Chapter 51
    The Questions 51
       Should the Researcher Use Self-Report or
         Non-Self-Report Measures? 51
       Who Should Do the Translating? 53
       Should the Translator Translate Literally? 54
       What Procedures Should the Translator Use? 55
       How Should the Researcher Test for Equivalence? 58
    A Concluding Note 61

Notes **62**

References **63**

About the Authors **70**

SERIES EDITOR'S INTRODUCTION

Nowadays scientific sample surveys of human populations—individuals in groups, organizations, communities, publics—are common. In almost every nation, it is an established social science methodology. While such surveys may be common within cultures, they have been relatively scarce across cultures. But that characterization is changing as the world grows smaller. More and more, researchers wish to apply the same survey instrument in two or more countries. A leading example is the Euro-Barometer, a nationwide public opinion survey regularly administered by the European Union in member countries since the 1970s. The task poses an obvious problem: how to ask the same question in X different languages, always retaining the same meaning? Of course, this issue is not confined to large multi-national projects. It comes up whenever a researcher wants to put in the field a questionnaire that was originally prepared in another language.

Poor translations of a survey instrument can render the data gathered from it valueless. But, important as it is, not enough attention is paid to rules for successful translation. This monograph will help change that. It carefully discusses steps to achieve semantic, conceptual, and normative equivalence when translating a questionnaire. Take, for instance, semantic equivalence. One should not merely hand the "source language" instrument to a native speaker and ask for a rewrite in the "target language," as is frequently done. This method, labelled "Simple Direct Translation," fares the worst of the six techniques reviewed, scoring "low" on informativeness, source language transparency, and security.

An alternative technique is "Modified Direct Translation," where the original translator meets with experts and they discuss the wording until they reach agreement. This procedure is not unusual. I followed it, for example, in preparing a survey on organizational innovation to be conducted in Peruvian hospitals. I translated my English questions into Spanish then discussed meaning and revisions with Peruvian social scientists, a Peruvian physician, and the local head of my interview team. The difficulty with such a procedure, as the authors explain, is that it is still not "high" on informativeness or source language transparency. The technique which scores high on these dimensions, higher than any other technique, is "Translation/Back-Translation," which involves bilingual individuals independently translating from source language to target and back, until agreement is reached.

Besides semantic equivalence, there are the problems of conceptual and normative equivalence. If a concept is the same from one culture to another, it should possess the same structure, according to Drs. Behling and Law. They note that factor analysis is a useful guide here, although they also caution that it should not be blindly followed. Take the concept of "political participation," much-studied by political scientists cross-culturally. Suppose that political participation means the same thing in country A and in country B. Then, a factor analysis of the items from the same scientific survey in each country should essentially yield the same dimensions, with the same defining items and loadings. Of course, as the authors wisely observe, this empirical equivalence may not occur in practice. Given that circumstance, one must ask if there are real conceptual differences in participation, or remaining methodological problems. Perhaps, for instance, there was a failure of normative equivalence, i.e., in country A political actions are openly discussed but in country B they are not. Thus, the responses in country B are biased and the survey results are of little utility for understanding political participation there.

Such methodological issues, as well as the nuances their interpretation requires, are nicely explicated in this practical primer on questionnaire translation. For researchers preparing to go abroad to administer a questionnaire in other than its original language, this is an especially important monograph to read. It may make all the difference in the success of their field work.

—Michael S. Lewis-Beck
Series Editor

ACKNOWLEDGMENT

James M. McFillen of Bowling Green State University made important contributions to the thinking on which this book is based. We acknowledge his contributions with gratitude.

TRANSLATING QUESTIONNAIRES AND OTHER RESEARCH INSTRUMENTS: PROBLEMS AND SOLUTIONS

ORLANDO BEHLING
Behling Associates

KENNETH S. LAW
Hong Kong University of Science and Technology

1. AN OVERVIEW

A query was posted on a research methods electronic bulletin board a few years ago. It read:

> Some colleagues and I need to translate a survey instrument into Chinese. The committee who is reviewing the submissions wants us to address the issue of "scale equating." We take this to mean that the translation must be done correctly, not only from the language perspective, but that we pick up the nuances, etc. that would allow our instrument to achieve validity, reliability, and possess the appropriate psychometric properties. Can anyone direct us to references that describe "scale equating?"

The plea generated a great deal of sympathy in one of the authors, who—along with several colleagues and students—was in the middle of a major effort to create workable Chinese, French, German, Japanese, and Korean versions of scales developed in U.S. English. He had found that a great deal of information exists, but that it is neither in one place nor in easily accessible form.

1

His concern for the problems created for researchers by the lack of a single, convenient source of information about translating research instruments, as well as his own frustration led to a presentation at the 1997 PanPacific Conference in Kuala Lumpur (Behling & McFillen, 1997). That presentation led in turn to this book.

Two Critical Questions

We must answer two critical questions before we can discuss the nuts and bolts of the translation process.

Should We Translate Questionnaires?

Important issues are currently being raised regarding the appropriateness of attempts to translate questionnaires and other paper-and-pencil measures both in academic disciplines (e.g., cultural anthropology and sociology) and in applied areas (e.g., marketing and management). Since the issues are laid out clearly in psychology, we focus on the "indigenous psychology movement" as an illustration.

The Indigenous Psychology Movement. The indigenous psychology movement has two faces.

First, it is a revolt against the domination of much of the world's social and behavioral sciences by Western—read American—conceptual frameworks and measures and a call for the development of concepts and measures based in local cultural realities. While emotionally loaded phrases such as "American psychological imperialism" (Gasquoine, 1997, p. 570) add more heat than light to the debate, the movement represents a needed and overdue challenge to the naïve assumption that American social and behavioral science can be exported around the world without considering unique aspects of target cultures.

Second, it is a supposition presented as a conclusion. Ho (1988) describes its most extreme form:

> In discussions about indigenization, one often encounters the following statement: Western psychology is simply irrelevant to and does not apply in Asia (or to Asians)... The argument typically runs as follows: Rooted in different cultural traditions, westerners and Asians differ in their thinking, feeling, and behavioral patterns. Hence we cannot rely on western psychology to understand Asians; we need to develop an

Asian psychology, separate from and independent of western psychology (p. 67).

Emic and Etic Conceptualizations. Berry (1969) makes a useful distinction between *etic* constructs—those that exist in identical or near identical form across a range of cultures—and *emic* constructs that are limited to a single culture. We can in fact find examples of Western ideas that are clearly emic as the advocates of indigenous psychologies argue. Hofstede and Bond (1988), for example, demonstrated that Hofstede's original four-dimensional conceptualization of national cultures (power distance, individualism/collectivism, masculinity/femininity, and uncertainity avoidance) lacks an element that is critical to Eastern thinking. This element, which they originally labeled "Confucian Dynamism," encompasses the values of persistence, status ordering of relationships, thrift, having a sense of shame, personal steadiness and stability, protecting "face," respect for tradition, and reciprocation of favors and gifts. Hofstede (1993) now labels a part of it "long-term versus short-term orientation."

But we can also find constructs that persist in recognizable form across very different cultures. For example, Ho (1998) points out that a norm of reciprocity—the belief that accepting a gift or favor entails an obligation to repay the giver—exists in almost all cultures, albeit sometimes in somewhat different forms. In a study of considerable interest to political scientists, Rubenstein (1996) demonstrated that Adorno's initially-Western construct of the authoritarian personality exists in very similar guise among both the Palestinian Moslems on the west bank of the Jordan River and among their Jewish neighbors in Israel, despite decades of bloody conflict.

Finally, Mitsumi and his colleagues [see Mitsumi & Peterson (1985) for an overview of the research stream] developed a PM (performance maintenance) leadership model in Japan that identifies two primary dimensions of leadership styles. *Performance leadership*, the "P" in the model, focuses on high quantity, high quality, fast work and adherence to rules. *Maintenance leadership* (M) emphasizes concern for the comfort and feelings of followers, reducing stress and expressing appreciation. These two dimensions strongly resemble ones uncovered decades earlier in the United States, e.g., *job-centered leadership* and *employee-centered leadership* (Likert, 1961) and, to a lesser degree, *consideration* and *initiation of structure* (Hemphill, 1950).

In sum, it appears to us as it does to other writers (e.g., Yang, 1997) that extreme versions of the indigenous psychology movement embody an error that is as worrisome as that built into the position that they are designed to replace. Assuming that there are *no* universals is as destructive as assuming that *all* Western ideas apply to all cultures throughout the world. The transferability of constructs and measures from one culture to another must be addressed on a case-by-case basis.

Can We Translate Questionnaires?

Three kinds of practical problems dog efforts to create meaningful target language equivalents of source language operationalizations.

Lack of Semantic Equivalence Across Languages. Lack of semantic equivalence across languages is our label for problems that hamper efforts to identify words and phrases in the target language that have meanings matching those in the source language instrument.

Merenda (1982) reports that he encountered several semantic problems in developing an Italian version of the Rhode Island Pupil Identification Scale (RIPIS), an instrument designed to help primary school teachers identify students with learning problems. The English language version of item 15, for example, reads simply that the student "Cries." Merenda (p. 132) points out:

> The straightforward translation to *piange* was correct. However, whereas teachers in the United States interpret this statement as intended, that is, as "cries excessively," Italian teachers evidently interpret it literally. Consequently, in the revised version an explanation of what is being called for was added to the item.

Similarly, Gielen (1982) found it necessary to append the following warning to his report of a study of differences in ideal self-images of German and U.S. university students:

> When interpreting the data...it is better to look at patterns among adjectives and not to be overconcerned with any specific adjective. It was often difficult to translate the Q-sort and it may well be that some adjectives have somewhat different connotations in the two languages. It is much less likely that these translation difficulties would have affected a whole pattern of adjective ratings (p. 286).

Lack of Conceptual Equivalence Across Cultures. Many instruments used in research across cultures are designed to operationalize constructs: formally defined concepts meaningful to members of the source culture. Problems associated with lack of conceptual equivalence across cultures have to do with the degree to which the concepts the researcher operationalizes in the source instrument—independent of the words and phrases used to represent them—exist in the same form in the thinking of members of the target culture. As Nowak (1976) asks:

> How do we know we are studying "the same phenomena" in different contexts; how do we know that our observations and conclusions do not actually refer to "quite different things," which we unjustifiably include into the same conceptual categories (p. 105)?

Lack of Normative Equivalence Across Societies. Each society has its own set of norms—social conventions—that exert powerful influences over many aspects of behavior. Those affecting three behaviors are of special importance to those translating research instruments.

Willingness to discuss certain topics: Societies vary markedly in the degree to which topics such as political opinions and family matters are discussed with strangers. Citizens of the People's Republic of China are less likely to be open regarding sexual behavior and political opinions, for example, than are their counterparts in Western Europe or North America.

Wierzbicka (1997) traces her personal odyssey from her native Poland to Australia, her adopted home. In her essay, she points out how Poles willingly discuss things English speakers often sidestep:

> The acute discomfort that [conversational routines such as "white lies" and "small talk"] were causing me led me to understand the value attached by Polish culture to "spontaneity," to saying what one really thinks, to talking about what one is really interested in, to showing what one really feels (p. 120).

Manner in which ideas are expressed: Societies vary in the way which answers may be given to questions. Specifically, the source and target societies may differ in the degree to which individuals show:

- Assertiveness versus acquiescence
- Self-enhancement versus modesty

- Objectivity versus social desirability
- Directness versus indirectness

Further, researchers may encounter society-to-society differences in a characteristic that Lonner (e.g., Lonner & Ibrahim, 1996) calls "positional response styles": the degree to which individuals consistently use the extremes in scales and other instruments.

Treatment of strangers: Reactions to strangers—particularly to strangers asking questions—also vary from society to society. Strangers are viewed with closed-mouth suspicion in some societies. Potential respondents are unwilling to open up to them. Other societies exhibit a norm of hospitality. Respondents are likely to be open with strangers, but may give answers that they believe will please the questioner rather than expressing true feelings or beliefs. In still other societies the role of the researcher is neither understood nor respected. Researchers' "silly" questions may lead respondents to see them as gullible or foolish. Respondents may feel free to feed them outrageous lies.

The Bottom Line

At first glance the formidable list of problems just outlined strikes many people as reason enough to abandon all attempts to use interviews and paper-and-pencil instruments outside their source language, culture, and society. As we explain in the following chapters, however, ways exist to deal with problems and to develop procedures and instruments that will yield useful information in most cases.

Suchman (1964), a sociologist, captures in a few words what we believe realistically can be accomplished, "A good design for the collection of comparative data should permit one to assume as much as possible that the differences observed... cannot be attributed to the differences in the method being used" (p. 135).

The ease with which a researcher can do this depends on several things. We believe that the most important is the nature of the information he or she seeks. Fyfe-Schaw (1995) points out that questionnaires are used to gather five major kinds of information[1]:

- **Background and Demographic Data.** A sprinkling of demographic questions is included in almost all questionnaires and interviewers' guides even if the researcher's main concern is not with accumulating facts about the respondents' age, sex, income, and other characteristics. Answers to them allow researchers to break the sample down into subgroups and, by doing so, to increase the value of their insights into responses to other questions.

- **Behavioral Reports.** Many researchers seek to understand the prevalence and frequency of particular behaviors. Questions may deal with behaviors that range from the socially desirable, e.g., "Did you vote in the last election?" or "How often do you attend church or synagogue?" through more-or-less neutral, e.g., "Which of the following brands of household cleaning products have you tried?" to the illegal, e.g., "Have you used marijuana in the last 30 days?"

- **Attitudes and Opinions.** Opinions may be thought of as judgments, most frequently about cause and effect relationships. For example, a researcher might ask, "Which of the following do you believe is the most important cause of crime in our nation?" Attitudes represent evaluations on a "good-to-bad" scale or some other dimension such as "satisfied-to-dissatisfied." Thus a researcher might ask, "Overall, on a scale of 1 to 10, where 1 equals very dissatisfied and 10 equals very satisfied, how satisfied are you with the job the government is doing in cleaning up the environment?"

- **Knowledge.** "Tests" provide a means of evaluating knowledge. Some attempt to gauge levels of awareness of topics or issues. For example, in the United States a researcher might ask, "What is the name of your representative in Congress?" Others may attempt to measure learning in courses or other educational experiences, e.g., "According to the authors of your textbook, what are the three most important elements of an effective law enforcement program?"

- **Intentions, Expectations, and Aspirations.** While intentions, expectations, and aspirations are obviously very different things, Fyfe-Shaw groups them together because all three deal with the future. Questions measuring them range from the relatively straightforward and innocuous, e.g., "Do you plan to buy a computer within the next 90 days?" through the more complex and socially loaded, e.g., "If the election were held today, for which of the following candidates would you vote?" to those involving difficult predictions, e.g., "What job do you expect to hold five years from now?"

Exhibit 1.1 summarizes our estimates of the risk of the three types of problems occurring when the researcher seeks one or another of the five types of information just discussed. The table contains major generalizations and simplifications—some might say overgeneralizations and oversimplifications—but we believe that it conveys useful

EXHIBIT 1.1

Relative Levels of the Three Kinds of Problems for Five Different Kinds of Information Researchers Seek

	Semantic	Conceptual	Normative
Background and Demographic Data	**Low:** With care, it is possible to pick target language words that yield correct facts.	**Low:** Concepts or constructs are not normally a part of demographic information	**High:** Societies vary in willingness to share various types of personal information with strangers.
Behavioral Reports	**Low:** It is generally quite easy to phrase questions in ways that clearly designate the behaviors of interest.	**Low:** Concepts or constructs are not normally a part of behavioral reports.	**High:** Societies vary widely in norms regarding what behaviors should be discussed with strangers.
Attitudes and Opinions	**High:** Attempts to find words that capture abstract ideas involved in measuring attitudes require extreme care.	**High:** Important questions have been raised about the universality of many concepts of interest to researchers.	**High:** Societies vary widely in attitudes and opinions that can properly be discussed with strangers.
Knowledge	**Medium:** Selecting wording that taps the same knowledge is difficult but not impossible.	**Low:** Concepts and constructs are not normally critical parts of measurement of knowledge.	**Low:** Questions are rarely culturally sensitive, though the tendency to become ego-involved in the "testing" process may vary from culture to culture.
Intentions, Expectations and Aspirations	**Medium:** Finding equivalent words for many intentions, expectations and aspirations is simple, but complex ones may be hard to translate.	**Low:** Questions about intentions, expectations and aspirations deal mostly with concrete items not abstract concepts.	**Medium:** Societies vary as to what intentions, expectations and aspirations may be discussed with strangers.

information about the nature and extent of the problems that researchers encounter in translating instruments that bear on the question "Can we translate questionnaires?"

First, the mix of problems facing the researcher varies depending on the kind of information sought. Those attempting to gather background and demographic data need to pay greatest attention to normative problems. Measurement of attitudes and opinions is threatened severely by all three kinds of problems. Attempts to gather information about respondents' knowledge and about their intentions, expectations, and aspirations encounter a mix of the three problems, though not at a high level.

Second, the overall difficulty of the job facing the researcher varies depending on the kind of information sought. In general we can say that seeking factual information with single questions creates the fewest problems while translating multi-item scales dealing with abstract concepts meets with the most.

2. CHARACTERISTICS OF USEFUL MEASURES

The translated version of a questionnaire or other research instrument must satisfy two sets of requirements. First, it must meet the basic standards set for all measures, translated or not. That is, it must be valid, reliable, legal, and cost-effective (i.e., possess utility). Second, it must meet requirements for equivalence relative to the source language measure. Not only must it possess acceptable levels of semantic and conceptual equivalence, but it and the procedures through which it is administered must also minimize problems created by lack of normative equivalence.

The researcher must determine and report the degree to which the target language instrument meets these two sets of requirements.

Basic Requirements

Many of the measures that researchers set out to translate have already been tested for reliability, validity, and utility in the source language. Satisfactory levels of these properties in the original instrument do not guarantee that the target language version will possess them as well, however. The researcher must determine and report the basic properties of the target language measure.

We describe these properties and identity some of the methods researchers use to test for them in the following paragraphs. The reader is referred to the numerous excellent books on the topic (e.g., DeVellis, 1991) for detailed discussions of the procedures involved.

Reliability

Reliability refers to the degree to which a measure of a construct is free from random error. It can be thought of as the correlation between a construct and itself. If a researcher were able to administer the same measure of a construct to the same individuals twice at the same instant, we would expect the correlation to equal 1.00. If it were found to be substantially less than 1.00, we would assume that some form of random error were present. But what if a researcher administers two different measures of the same construct (source and target language versions of a voter attitude scale, for example), one proven, and the other not? If the unproven measure truly taps the same variable as the proven version, theoretically the correlation should equal 1.00. If the correlation is substantially less, error must be present, presumably in the unproven measure. Thus, tests of reliability typically involve correlating two different measurements of the same construct.

Researchers usually report the results of one or more of three kinds of tests of reliability: parallel forms, test-retest, and internal consistency.

Parallel Forms Reliability. Researchers correlate sources obtained on two different measures of the same construct (e.g., "Form A" and "Form B" of a test of intelligence) to determine parallel forms reliability. Parallel forms reliability is relatively easy to determine when both Form A and Form B are in the same language. One administers both forms to a sample of respondents and calculates a simple product-moment correlation. Parallel forms reliability is calculated in several different ways. They differ mainly in their interpretation of the error component in the measurement.

The process becomes more complicated when the two forms are in different languages (e.g., Form B is a Spanish language version of a questionnaire originally written in English). The special problems that dog the researcher in this case are considered in detail in the next chapter. We discuss several examples there.

Test-Retest Reliability. Researchers determine the level of test-retest reliability by administering the same measure to the same individuals at two different times. The researcher then calculates a product-moment correlation coefficient using the scores from the two administrations. Referred to as the "coefficient of stability," the result provides an index of test-retest reliability.

Internal Consistency Reliability. If a scale used to measure a construct contains more than one item, it can be divided in the two halves. Each half can be considered a parallel form, albeit a shortened one. The correlation between these two halves, referred to logically enough as split-half reliability, can be used to estimate a scale's reliability. For a scale consisting of k items, there are $.5 \, _kC_{k/2}$ different possible split-halves. The average of all these estimated possible split-half reliabilities constitutes the coefficient alpha of the measure. It is widely used as an index of internal consistency reliability.

Reliability of Translated Measures. Concern for culture-to-culture variations in the reliability of measures is not unwarranted. For example, researchers (e.g., Lonner & Ibrahim, 1996) consistently report that individuals in Far Eastern cultures are (a) more likely to select a more-or-less neutral midpoint from among a set of response alternatives and (b) less likely to give negative responses than are their Western counterparts. These response sets reduce the observed variance of scores on translated scales. Guthrie (1961) reports that mothers studied in an attempt to understand child-rearing practices in the Philippines also tended to give positive responses. The true score variance may not be affected, since the reduction in observed variance is an artifact. The net result is, therefore, an overestimation of the true reliability of the translated version of the scale. Similarly, where respondents have a tendency to use extreme scores, reliability can be underestimated.

Validity

Validity is the degree to which a measure is free from systematic bias. Nunnally (1978) identifies three forms of validity: predictive validity, content validity, and construct validity.

Predictive Validity. Nunnally (1978) suggests that "Predictive validity is at issue when the purpose is to use an instrument to estimate some important form of behavior that is external to the measuring instrument itself, the latter being known as the *criterion*" (p. 8). Tests of predictive validity generally begin with the criterion. Possible predictors are identified and tested to determine if they do in fact relate clearly to it. Predictive validity is present if the measuring instrument accurately predicts the criterion.

Take the hypothetical case of a researcher who has obtained a grant to demonstrate the effectiveness of a program to prevent alcohol abuse among high school students. Singling out those students who are at risk so that they can receive help before they become abusers could well be a key part of the project. In this example, a questionnaire could be said to have predictive validity if it accurately identifies students at risk for future abuse. Similarly, a new attitude measure might be tested for its usefulness as a predictor of voter behavior or a measure of employee satisfaction might be tested by determining if it separates those employees who leave the firm within the next six months from those who remain.

Barrick and Mount (1991) performed a meta-analysis demonstrating that a personality dimension called conscientiousness was an excellent predictor of three criteria (job performance, training performance, and personnel information, such as supervisory ratings) across five different occupational groups. The usefulness of their results was constrained by the fact that all of the studies examined were performed in North America. Salgado (1997) performed a similar meta-analysis using studies performed within the European Union that revealed generally comparable results. Clearly, Salgado's work extends the predictive validity of the measures used across languages, cultures, and societies.

Content Validity. Content validity refers to the adequacy with which a measure samples the realm of interest. As Nunnally (1978) points out, "For some instruments, validity depends primarily on the adequacy with which a specific domain of content is sampled" (p. 9). A final examination in a research methods course has content validity if it contains an appropriate mix of questions tapping all key areas of the course, for example.

Chen's (1997) test of Becker's concept of commitment to supervisor (Becker, Billings, Eveleth, & Gilbert, 1996) provides an example of culture-to-culture differences in content validity. The construct as operationalized in the original English language instrument has two dimensions: *identification with the supervisor* and *internalization of his or her values*. However, Chen found three more dimensions of the construct among Chinese: *dedication of the subordinate to the supervisor; effort*, which is the subordinate's willingness to exert effort on behalf of his/her supervisor; and *following supervisor*, which is the subordinate's intention to stay with the supervisor as circumstances change. Chen argues that a direct translation of Becker's original instrument provides incomplete coverage of the construct's domain in China.

Construct Validity. Construct validity refers to the accuracy with which an observable (e.g., a person's score on the Manifest Anxiety Scale) reflects the unobservable latent variable or construct that it purports to represent (in this example, the person's "actual" level of anxiety).

Nunnally (1978) proposes a three-step procedure for testing for construct validity. The researcher should first list out all the observables that may act as surrogates for the construct. He or she should then determine if in fact they all measure the same thing. Finally, he or she should determine empirically, "...whether a supposed measure of a construct correlates in expected ways with measures of other constructs or is affected in expected ways by particular experimental treatments" (p. 98).

If a translated scale possesses predictive validity, scores obtained using it relate to measures of other constructs in one of two patterns. First, they may exhibit the same pattern as the source language original. Second, they may relate in ways that differ from those found in the source language, but that are expected based upon understanding of differences between the source and target languages, cultures, and societies.

Cheung and Bagley (1998) provide evidence of the construct validity of a Chinese language version of the Center for Epidemiological Studies Depression Scale, which was originally written in English. They do so by showing that the depressive symptoms scale and the interpersonal problems scale that make it up relate as predicted. Paunonen and Ashton (1998), on the other hand, report that scores on the Personality Research Form and the Nonverbal Personality Questionnaire—two instruments that purport to measure the same variables—did not correlate as highly as expected in a second language. They attribute the lack of construct validity to a combination of poor translation and cultural differences.

Utility

The utility of a measurement scale can be conceptualized in three ways: statistical significance, practical utility, and economic utility.

Statistical Significance. In some cases a measurement is considered useful when results indicate that there is a high probability that a correlation between the variable it measures and one or more others in its nomological net is significantly greater than zero. Researchers, of course, often test for statistical significance. Evidence of a statistically significant relationship between variables may be used, for example, as evidence to support a hypothesis.

Practical Utility. By one definition, practical utility refers to the proportion of the variance in the dependent variable explained by a measure. For example, suppose a researcher determined that the correlation between a measure of voter satisfaction and the likelihood that an individual would vote for the party in power was .15. This means voter satisfaction accounts for slightly more than 2 percent of the variance in voter choice. It is, assuming statistical significance for the figure, a predictor of behavior. By a second definition, practical utility is a judgment made by a potential user of the information. Most individuals would conclude that the practical utility of a relationship that accounts for only 2 percent of the variance is small.

Researchers' judgments of practical utility may change from one society to another because practical utility can be assessed only with knowledge of the availability of alternative predictors. In marketing programs, for example, a predictor that correlates .20 with a criterion may not be of much interest if predictors with much higher validity are available. However, it this were the only valid predictor of buyer behavior identified in a given society, a sales manager might be happy to use it.

Economic Utility. Economic utility refers to evaluation of a scale's cost/benefit ratio. Economic utility may be an important consideration for applied researchers. The cost of gathering information has to be weighed against its benefits in order to decide if using an interview or a paper-and-pencil measure is an efficient way to assess the variable of concern.

The ratio of costs to benefits varies from society to society. Setting up a costly system to perform telephone surveys in countries where few households have phones would almost certainly be a poor investment for a market researcher, for example. If the literacy rate in a country is low or the postal service is slow and unreliable, the cost of gathering information via a mailed-in questionnaire may outweigh the potential benefits. First, response rates will probably be low. Second, because there is no way to find out if those who did respond really understood the items or instructions, important questions can be raised about the interpretation of the data. Structured interviews may provide a more cost-effective alternative.

Legality

Legality and its sibling cultural acceptability impose important constraints on the design of questionnaires and other research instruments.

Definitions of what is considered "sensitive information" differ widely from society to society. Concern for things such as personal privacy, free expression of political views, and discrimination against ethnic, religious, gender, sexual preference, and age groups differs across cultures. For example, Chinese commonly ask questions about others' personal and family lives; such inquiries are perceived as expressions of concern for the other person. The same questions are seen as invasions of privacy by many Westerners. In some countries only information proven to be predictive of future job performance may be included in a selection interview or questionnaire. In other countries there are few if any legal limits on what may be asked.

Equivalence

Demonstrating that a translated questionnaire possesses the basic characteristics required of all measurement instruments is not enough. In addition, the researcher must show that it exhibits appropriate levels of semantic and conceptual equivalence relative to the source language measure and that it and the procedures through which it is administered minimize any problems created by lack of normative equivalence.

Semantic Equivalence

Semantic equivalence involves the choice of terms and sentence structures that ensure that the meaning of the source language statement is preserved in the translation. We discuss procedures for assuring semantic equivalence in Chapter 3.

Conceptual Equivalence

Conceptual equivalence refers to the degree to which a concept, independent of the words used to operationalize it, exists in the same form in the source and target cultures. We discuss procedures for assuring conceptual equivalence in Chapter 4.

Normative Equivalence

Normative equivalence refers to the degree to which the researcher has dealt successfully with the problems created by differences in societal rules dealing with:

- The openness with which particular topics are discussed
- The manner in which ideas are expressed
- The way in which strangers, particularly strangers asking questions, are treated

We discuss means for managing it in Chapter 5.

3. SOLVING SEMANTIC PROBLEMS

The Nature of Semantic Problems

Semantic problems have to do with the identification of words and phrases in the target language that have meanings identical or similar to those used in the source language instrument.

Dealing with semantic problems looks simple at first glance, but it can turn out to be quite challenging. Saito, Nomuro, Noguchi, and Tezuka's (1996) efforts to develop a Japanese language version of the Family Environment Scale illustrate the difficulty of the decisions that translators must make when seeking semantic equivalence:

> [We] replaced "The Bible is a very important book in our home" (in English) with "Religious items (family shrine, Buddhist altar, Bible) are very important in our home" (in Japanese). "Family members attend church, synagogue, or Sunday School fairly often" was translated into "My family often participates in religious meetings and events" (p. 244).

How perfectly the words and phrases Saito et al. chose convey the meanings of the English originals is open to debate. We can simplify the job of solving problems of semantic equivalence, however, if we recognize that the task facing the translator creating a target language equivalent of an existing instrument differs from that facing the researcher creating a brand new one.

Solving Semantic Problems When Translating an Existing Instrument

Guthery and Lowe (1992) identify six methods researchers use to prepare target language versions of existing instruments. They are: direct translation, which we divide into simple direct translation and modified direct translation; translation/back-translation; the ultimate test; the parallel blind technique; the random probe technique; and decentering.[2] Decentering is discussed in the next section. We describe the others in the following paragraphs and evaluate them in terms of four criteria:

- **Informativeness.** The degree to which the technique provides the researcher with objective indications of the semantic equivalence of the target language version of the instrument and pinpoints the nature of specific problems with it.

- **Source Language Transparency.** The degree to which the technique provides useful information to the researcher who lacks fluency in the target language. Frequently the primary investigator or the author of the original instrument does not read or write the target language well. Yet he or she is called upon to make key decisions about the translated instrument and interpret the data gathered with it. Thus, ideally, a translation technique should yield its information in a form that allows a monolingual researcher to understand and solve problems with the target language instrument and to properly interpret results obtained using it.

- **Security.** The degree to which the technique builds in opportunities to check the work of the original translator. Allowing other bilingual individuals to examine the translator's choices or allowing comparisons of back-translated versions to the original source language items increases confidence in the accuracy of the translation, for example.

- **Practicality.** The degree to which the technique yields a finished target language instrument quickly, cheaply, and easily.

EXHIBIT 3.1

Authors' Judgment of the Degree to Which Each of the Six
Techniques Meets the Four Criteria for a Useful Technique

	Informative-ness	Source Language Transparency	Security	Practicality
Simple Direct Translation	Low	Low	Low	High
Modified Direct Translation	Medium	Medium	Medium	Low
Translation/ Back-Translation	High	High	Medium	Medium
Parallel Blind Technique	Medium	Medium	High	Medium
Random Probe	Medium	Low	Low	High
"Ultimate" Test	High	Low	High	Low

Exhibit 3.1 summarizes our judgments of the degree to which the six
techniques meet the various criteria for a useful technique for creating
a target language version of an existing instrument.

Simple Direct Translation

In simple direct translation, a bilingual individual translates the instrument from the source language into the target language—period,
end of sentence. This technique is practical; the results can be obtained quickly and cheaply. Simple direct translation does not score
well on the other criteria, however. It is not informative; it generates no objective information about the quality of the translation or
specific problems with it. Since the quality of the target language
version depends strictly upon a lone translator's skill and judgment,
security is low. The monolingual researcher is provided with no infor-

mation regarding the quality of the final instrument or the nature of any potential problems with it. Thus source language transparency is also low.

Modified Direct Translation

Geisinger (1994) presents a ten-step procedure that overcomes some of our concerns with simple direct translation. Most importantly, he recommends independent checks on the work of the original translator by a panel of experts who review the draft target language instrument. He proposes that they "(a) review the items and react in writing, (b) share their comments with one another, and (c) meet to consider the points made by each other and to reconcile any differences of opinion" (p. 306). He argues that the original translator should meet with the panel twice. In the first meeting, panel members explain their concerns. In the second meeting: "The translator or adapter can ... explain the reasons for drafting the instrument in the manner used. Similarly, the panel can explain why they reacted to the draft as they did" (p. 306).

Discussions among the panel members and between panel members and the translator make modified direct translation more informative than simple, direct translation. Reliance on the judgment of a panel of experts substantially increases security as well. However, the researcher should recognize that the panel is not a perfect guarantee of security. The panel members may in fact be no more competent or even less competent than the original translator. Also, given the well-documented problems involved in obtaining a truly representative consensus through group discussion, the researcher has no assurance that the panel will arrive at the best possible translation.

If the monolingual primary investigator or scale author sits in on the discussions—assuming they are held in the source language— Geisinger's modification leads to substantial source language transparency. Practicality is relatively low, however. The technique is likely to consume substantial amounts of time, effort, and money.

Translation/Back-Translation

In its most basic form, translation/back-translation is an iterative process in which each cycle involves four steps:

1. A bilingual individual translates the source language instrument into the target language.

2. A second bilingual individual with no knowledge of the wording of the original source language document translates this draft target language rendering back into the source language.
3. The original and back-translated source language versions are compared.
4. If substantial differences exist between the two source language documents, another target language draft is prepared containing modifications designed to eliminate the discrepancies.

The process is repeated until the two source language documents are identical or contain only minor differences. Saito et al. (1996) provide an example of how the translation/back-translation process works. One of the original English items making up the Family Environment Scale reads as follows:

It's hard to be yourself without hurting someone's feelings in our household (p. 245).

The first rendering in Japanese was back-translated as:

In my family we have to be careful of a certain person's feelings, which leaves him/her isolated from the rest of us (p. 245).

Since the two English versions of the item differed substantially, a second translation was attempted. This was back-translated as:

In my family, as we have to be careful of a certain person's feelings, it is difficult for me to be alone (p. 245).

The authors concluded that, while this did not match for the original English statement perfectly, the differences were not great enough to justify a third iteration.

Translation/back-translation contains a "seat of the pants" element. No one has specified an objective rule for deciding how close is "close enough" when comparing original and back-translated source language items. However, it scores well in terms of informativeness, source language transparency, and security.

The ability to compare the back-translated version to the original source language version is a major contributor to the informativeness of the technique. It should be noted, however, that at least four factors can lead to similarity of original and back-translated source language versions when in fact the target language rendering does not represent the ideas in the source language document well. Brislin (1970) first identified three of them:

1. The individuals doing the "forward" and back-translations may apply the same set of conventions for handling material that is in fact not equivalent.
2. Some back-translators may be able to make sense out of a target language version of a statement even if it depicts the original ideas poorly. The individual responsible for the back-translation may be able to guess the intent of a poorly translated item if he or she is knowledgeable about the concepts underlying it. Thus he or she may come up with a back-translated version that is misleadingly close to the original source language wording.
3. Even though the translated item may be unintelligible or nonsensical to a target language speaker, the draft target language version may contain elements of the source language grammatical structure that make it possible for a bilingual individual to guess the source wording.

Hambleton (1993) (cited in Geisinger, 1994) identifies a fourth point that should be added to Brislin's list:

4. "[W]hen translators knew that their work was going to be subjected to back translation, they would use wording that ensured that a second translation would faithfully reproduce the original version rather than a translation using the optimal wording in the target language" (Geisinger, 1994, p. 306).

Translation/back-translation has substantial source language transparency. The monolingual researcher can compare original and back-translated source language versions of items, permitting him or her to play a major role in the development of the instrument and to better understand the data obtained. Though it does not directly identify the source of specific problems, it calls attention to troublesome items, thus rating high in informativeness. It also rates high in security since it allows intense discussion of individual items among the researcher and the two translators.

The need for two translators increases the cost and the multistep process can result in substantial time passing before the final version is available. Thus we rate translation/back-translation as intermediate in practicality.

Ultimate Test

Brislin (1973) suggests a two-part procedure for testing for semantic equivalence. The first, which he labels the "performance criterion," can be used if the material of concern asks for some action on the reader's part. He states, "The subject may be requested to perform a task with the target language version as the instructions. If he can complete the task, the original and target language versions are undoubtedly equivalent" (p. 53).

In the second half of the ultimate test, bilingual individuals are randomly assigned to four groups. Members of the first group respond to the source language version of the scale. Members of the second group respond to the draft target language version of the scale. Members of the remaining groups respond to "split" versions. The third group receives instruments in which the first half of the items is in the source language and the second half in the target language. The fourth group responds to a version of the scale in which the first half is in the target language and the second half in the source language.

Responses are compared in two ways. First, the mean total scores and item frequency distributions among the four groups of respondents are compared. Brislin considers absence of statistically significant differences to be evidence that the draft translation represents the source language version adequately. Second, the researcher calculates correlations between scores on the "source language" and "target language" halves of the questionnaires given to the third and fourth groups. High positive correlations support the conclusion that the target language version accurately represents the source language original.

A major advantage of the ultimate test lies in the area of security. It provides objective indications (significant correlations between scores for the halves and insignificant differences among the mean scores for the four groups) of comparability. It should be recognized, however, that such indications could result from many things, of which equivalence is only one. Thus these results are necessary but not sufficient grounds for accepting the source and target language versions as semantically equivalent.

The ultimate test has four limitations. Two are simple mechanical ones. The first of the two tests can be used only when specific behavioral response is called for. The second of the two tests can be used only when multi-item scales are used. While this is common in attitude measurement and personality assessment, such redundancy may not be present when gathering other kinds of information. Second, in terms of practicality, it requires what many researchers will find to be a prohibitively large number of qualified bilingual individuals. Third, the "ultimate" test conveys a relatively small amount of information. A significant positive correlation or a lack of differences in means may hide important problems with individual items. The opposite—significant differences in mean scores or the absence of significant correlations—tells the researcher that a problem exists, but provides no guidance as to what it is or how to solve it. That is, it does not direct attention to a particular item or items.

Parallel Blind Technique

Werner and Campbell (1970) identify a technique in which two translators independently prepare versions of the draft target language instrument. They then meet to compare their versions and to resolve any differences. Once they do so, they jointly present the target language instrument to the researcher.

Guthery and Lowe (1992) argue that the parallel blind technique has two advantages: speed, an element of what we label "practicality," and researcher control, an element of what we label "source language transparency." The process is faster than conventional translation/back-translation because the two translators work in parallel rather than in sequence. Also, checking the two translations against one another provides an element of security.

On the negative side, the parallel blind technique lacks a second aspect of what we call source language transparency. That is, unless the researcher is fluent in the two languages, he or she can play only a limited role in the translation process. He or she cannot know if, for example, the translators share certain misconceptions or if what appears to be agreement between them stems from unwillingness to criticize one another's translations.

Random Probe Technique

The random probe technique calls for the researcher to administer the draft target language instrument to a group of target language speakers who are then asked to explain why they responded as they did to individual items. According to Guthery and Lowe (1992), "If the respondent's justification for the original answer is strange, then the intent of the question is not being conveyed" (p. 10). The technique is cheap, simple, and quick—practical, in other words. However, because it involves little more than asking the respondents an open-ended question, researchers will most likely find it useful as a supplement to or as a part of a more rigorous procedure. It provides only limited information and is not innately source language transparent.

Solving Semantic Problems When Creating a New Instrument

Sometimes, either by choice or by necessity, researchers create new instruments for use in two or more languages. In this section we start by discussing a general recommendation for doing this: write with translation in mind. We then describe three alternative procedures—source language centering, decentering, and the multilingual team approach—for the creation of comparable instruments and rate them in terms of the same four criteria we used to evaluate the techniques for translating existing instruments.

Write with Translation in Mind

Some research instruments are easier to translate than others are. In part this reflects differences in the information researchers seek or the constructs they wish to operationalize. Researchers can frame questions about some topics in relatively simple, easy-to-translate ways. Other information can be teased out only through complicated, difficult-to-translate questions. As explained in Exhibit 1.1, items requesting factual information (e.g., background and demographics and behavioral reports) are likely to present fewer problems for the translator than those dealing with attitudes and opinions.

Brislin (1973, 1980) argues that difficulties encountered in developing multiple versions of a single instrument stem from more than the nature of the information sought, however. He believes that researchers can make the task easier by using proper words, grammatical forms, and sentence structures. He encapsulates his advice in twelve rules. The italicized sentences (emphasis supplied) at the beginning of each paragraph are taken from Brislin (1980). The remainder of each paragraph is ours.

1. *Use short, simple sentences of less than sixteen words.* Miller (1991) presents an item from Adorno, Frenkel-Bruswik, Levinson, and

Stanford's Authoritarian Personality Scale, "What this country needs most, more than laws and political programs, is a few tireless, devoted leaders in whom the people can put their faith" (p. 513). A less convoluted sentence would pose fewer problems for the development of parallel versions in other languages. While far from ideal, writing it as, "This country needs tireless, devoted leaders in whom the people can put their faith more than this country needs laws and political programs" would certainly help.

2. *Employ the active rather than the passive voice.*[3] The active voice expresses a thought in a more straightforward manner than does the passive voice. Compare, for example, two items from the scale Neal and Seeman (Miller, 1991, pp. 472–473) developed to measure powerlessness (low expectancies for control over the political system, the economy, and international affairs), a variable of considerable interest to some political scientists. One item is in the active voice. It reads (reverse scored), "People like me can change the course of world events if we make ourselves heard" (p. 473). Another in the passive voice reads, "There's very little we can do to keep prices from going higher" (p. 473). Translators are more likely to be able to create equivalent versions of the former than of the latter.

3. *Repeat nouns rather than using pronouns.* Wollack, Goodale, Wijting, and Smith (1971) developed a scale that contains the following item, "A person should hold a second job to bring in extra money if the person can get it" (p. 336). While it is obvious to most readers of the English language version that "it" refers to a "second job" not to "extra money," rewriting the question to read, "A person should hold a second job to bring in extra money if the person can get such a job" would make the referent absolutely clear to any future translator.

4. *Avoid metaphor and colloquialisms.* The Social Support for Transactions Questionnaire (SSQT) (Suurmeijer *et al.*, 1995) was developed as a part of a program aimed at determining the role social support plays in patients' health facilitation and stress reduction and in amelioration of the negative effects of events. Some SSQT items contain traps for those developing parallel versions in other languages. A careful look at two items illustrates the nature of those traps. Item 5 reads, "Does it ever happen to you that people are willing to lend you a friendly ear?" (p. 1229). Item 8 reads, "Does it ever happen to you that people give you a nudge in the right direction, as it were?" (p. 1229).

Idioms such as "lend an ear" meaning listen sympathetically and "nudge in the right direction" meaning subtly helping one choose the proper course of action and qualifiers such as "as it were" are among the last things a non-native speaker learns. Few translators can be expected to have mastered all or even most of those used by fluent source language writers.

Also, they present even the most skilled translator with a difficult choice. He or she may translate the idiom literally (the possibilities inherent in a literal translation of "lend an ear" are fascinating) or attempt to select an equivalent but different target language metaphor or colloquialism or abandon the use of metaphor or colloquialism entirely and use a standard denotative definition of the term the idiom represents. While the third alternative is probably the least undesirable of the three, none of the them is totally satisfactory. The obvious solution is, as Brislin recommends, avoiding the use of colloquialisms and metaphors in the first place.

5. *Avoid the subjunctive mood, e.g., verb forms with "could" or "would."* The subjunctive mood, which expresses wishes or conditions contrary to fact (e.g., "If you were President of the United States in what three areas would you cut spending?") does not exist in all languages. Even if it does, it may be difficult to express in the target language.

However, valuable as it is, we go a step beyond Brislin's advice. We recommend that researchers avoid all but the simplest sentence constructions whenever possible. Some auxiliary verb forms ("Do you believe your representative *ought to vote* for the bill?" "Is this statement true or false, I *might vote* for her if she runs for office") create problems for translators. The same can be said of various progressive tenses (e.g., the progressive passive "*Are* you *being bothered* by phone calls from telemarketers?") and perfect tenses (e.g., the past perfect, "*Had you been called* more than three times a day?").

6. *Add sentences which provide context for key ideas. Reword key phrases to provide redundancy.* Though Brislin does not explicitly define "context" and "redundancy," the former appears to refer to adding phrases or sentences to individual items or repeating in different words an idea that might otherwise be difficult to understand. House and Rizzo (1972) provide an example of context in a scale they developed to measure job-related anxiety and stress. Item 17 reads, "I often 'take my job home with me,' in the sense that I think about it while doing other things" (p. 501). By repeating the idea they wish to convey, House and Rizzo increase the likelihood that any future translator will accurately grasp their intended meaning. Redundancy refers to the use of multiple items to represent a single construct. Though a translator may misinterpret an individual item, the chance is small that he or she will make the same error in several items.

7. *Avoid adverbs and prepositions telling "where" or "when" (e.g., frequent, beyond, upper).* The use of words and phrases specifying place and number frequently requires the translator to provide equivalents to terms

that are defined fuzzily in the source language. Parry and Warr (1980) developed the Home Role Scale, which is designed to tap women's attitudes toward household duties and childcare. It contains the following two items: "I feel my family takes me too much for granted" (p. 249) and "I wish my children showed their love for me more" (p. 249). Developing a parallel version of their scale would be much easier if the translator were not required to find target language equivalents of "too much" and "more."

8. *Avoid possessive forms when possible.* A fictitious item that might appear in a political scientist's investigation of sources of information swaying voter behavior might read: "My newspaper provides complete and unbiased coverage of local political races." It would be easier to translate were it phrased to eliminate the possessive form, which introduces an element of vagueness. For example, it might be phrased, "Does the newspaper you read most frequently provide complete and unbiased coverage of local political races?"

9. *Use specific rather than general terms (e.g., the specific animal such as cows, chickens, pigs, rather than the general term "livestock").* Kalleberg, Knoke, Marsden, and Spaeth (1996) wrote a set of items designed to collect information about business firms' levels of formalization (the degree to which written documentation exists governing key personnel-related processes) as part of an interviewer's guide. They chose to ask eight questions, each having to do with a specific kind of documentation, the first dealing with a "rules and procedures manual," the second with written job descriptions, the third with written records of job performance, and so on. Obviously, Kalleberg *et al.* made a translator's task simpler than it would have been if they had chosen to ask a single question dealing with the degree or level of use of written documentation of personnel-related processes.

10. *Avoid words indicating vagueness regarding some event or thing (e.g., probably and frequently).* Price (1997, pp. 465–466), designed an eight-item scale to measure prestige stratification in organizations. The eight items contain, respectively, the following vague qualifiers: "generally," "mostly," "usually," "often," "generally," "usually," "typically," and "usually." For example, item 3 reads, "Managers and non-managers are usually on a first-name basis." This scale may be a useful tool in English (it had not been tested for reliability and validity at the time of original publication), but the qualifiers create problems for translators who must find target language equivalents.

11. *Use wording familiar to the translators where possible.* Brislin (1970) reports the results of research demonstrating that unfamiliar words create difficulties for translators. In this study bilingual college students

translated English language materials written at two levels of difficulty (third grade English versus seventh grade English) into ten non-Indo-European languages. Other bilingual students translated the results back into English. Comparisons of the back-translated versions with the English language originals revealed that a lower level of difficulty yielded significantly more accurate translations.

12. *Avoid sentences with two different verbs if the verbs suggest two different actions.* Georgopoulos and Mann (1962) developed a scale to measure coordination in hospitals. Item 1 asks, "How well do the different jobs and work activities around the patient fit together, or how well are all things geared in the direction of giving good patient care?" (p. 290). Breaking the one item into two would simplify the translator's task.

Writing with translation in mind makes the translator's task easier. Alone, however, it does not guarantee the equivalence of target and source language versions of a research instrument.

Three Approaches to Solving Semantic Problems When Creating a New Instrument

We describe three techniques for solving semantic problems when starting from scratch in the following paragraphs: source language centering, decentering, and the multicultural team approach. We then evaluate them in terms of the same four criteria that we used to evaluate techniques for translating existing instruments. Exhibit 3.2 provides a rough summary of our judgment of the performance of the three techniques on the four criteria for a useful technique for creating equivalent target language and source language versions of a new instrument.

Source Language Centering. In source language centering, the researcher authors an instrument in the source language. He or she then translates it into the target language, using some mix of the procedures suggested in the section headed, "Solving Semantic Problems When Using Existing Instruments." Source language centering is the simplest and, sadly, the most commonly used approach. We say "sadly" because it treats the problem without recognizing the unique opportunities developing an instrument from scratch presents to the cross-cultural researcher. Two procedures—decentering and the cross-cultural team approach—provide important advantages.

Decentering. Decentering (Brislin, 1973) is "a translation process in which the source and the target language versions are equally impor-

EXHIBIT 3.2
Authors' Judgment of the Degree to Which Each of the Three
Techniques Meets the Four Criteria for a Useful Technique

	Informative-ness	Source Language Transparency	Security	Practicality
Source Language Centering	High	High	Low	Medium
Decentering	High	High	High	Low
Multicultural Team Approach	High	Medium	Low	Low

tant and [equally] open to modification during the translation process"
(pp. 37–38). Clearly, this broad definition allows for several different
forms of decentering. Indeed, it may be more useful to think of it as
an approach rather than as a specific technique.

Nevertheless, we present one procedure as an example of decentering. As examination of the steps listed below indicates, this version
of decentering is, in effect, translation/back-translation with a special
twist. It consists of the following steps:

1. The researcher develops a source language instrument.
2. A bilingual individual translates it into the target language.
3. A second bilingual individual with no knowledge of the content of the
   original source language instrument translates this draft instrument back
   into the source language.
4. The original and back-translated source language versions are compared.
5. If substantial differences exist between the two source language documents, changes designed to eliminate the discrepancies are made in
   the wording of the source language instrument, the target language instrument, or both. In some cases, the back-translated version is simply
   substituted for the original source language item. Both the source language and the target language versions are equally subject to change.
6. This process is repeated using other translators until identical or near
   identical source and target language versions are obtained.

Brislin (1973, pp. 38–39) explains how he translated the Marlow–Crowne Social Desirability Scale (Crowne & Marlow, 1964) into Chamorro, the language of Guam and the Marianas Islands, as an example of decentering. Item 18 read, "I don't find it particularly difficult to get along with loud-mouthed, obnoxious people" in English. Since there were no Chamorro equivalents of "particularly" and "obnoxious," the back-translator omitted them. A revised English item was translated into Chamorro by a third bilingual individual and back-translated by a fourth. The later changed it slightly, arguing that the Chamarro equivalent of "talk with" would be easier for the target population to understand than "get along with." As a result, the final English version of the item reads, "It is not hard for me to talk with people who have a big mouth."

Decentering has a number of advantages. Like translation/back-translation, it is both informative and source language transparent. It also provides the researcher with an opportunity to check the thinking of one translator against another, thus rating high in security. It rates low in practicality, however, since it requires a substantial number of translators and the iterative nature of the process may eat up considerable time.

Multicultural Team Approaches. Greenfield (1997) advocates a relatively conservative form of multicultural team approach. She argues that:

> ... it is best to have a bicultural (or multicultural) team and to collaboratively develop a single instrument for all cultures before the study begins ... egalitarian, multicultural collaboration in instrument development constitutes a powerful tool to detect and prevent the cross-cultural misunderstandings that undermine validity in cross-cultural ability testing (p. 1117).

Others advocate a more radical version of the multicultural team approach, which we refer to as the "Triandis procedure," because Professor Harry Triandis and his colleagues at the University of Illinois developed it (see, for example, Davidson, Jaccard, Triandis, Morales, & Dias-Guerrero, 1976).

The Triandis procedure for item development neatly sidesteps the issue of translation. It does so by creating parallel operationalizations in the target and source languages at the same time, rather than creating the source language version first and then deriving the target language version from it. The researcher begins with a construct assumed to be *etic* and then enlists natives of the target culture to identify *emic* manifestations of it in their language. Items are not only created by members of a particular culture, but well may be unique to it. That is, though items may tap the same construct, they may bear little or no relationship to one another in terms of wording, format, or even subject matter.

The multicultural team approaches have the potential to be highly informative. The discussions among the team members provide excellent forums for the exchange of ideas and the development of insights into the various cultures and forms of the instrument. Multicultural team approaches are not innately source language transparent, nor do they provide means of formally cross-checking the choices made by target language experts. The most telling problem has to do with their lack of practically, however. They are likely to be extremely costly and time consuming.

4. SOLVING CONCEPTUAL PROBLEMS

Finding solutions to semantic problems is necessary to ensure the quality of a translation. It is not sufficient, however. The researcher must also deal with problems of conceptual equivalence: those that occur when the concept operationalized in the source instrument—independent of the words and phrases used to represent it—does not exist in the same form in the thinking of members of the target culture.

Take the idea of self-concept. "Self" refers to the individual human being in individualistic cultures such as the United States. Western self-concept scales (e.g., Shavelson, Hubner, & Stanton, 1976) reflect that fact. It can be argued, however, that a person in a collectivistic culture such as Japan should find it difficult to separate her or his identity from that of her or his family or even from that of the firm in which he or she works. If this is the case, the Western idea of self-concept and instruments designed to measure it capture only a part of the construct at best.

Identifying and solving conceptual problems require both logical analysis and empirical tests.

Logical Tests of Conceptual Equivalence

Any effort to solve conceptual problems should begin with careful consideration of:

- The constitutive definitions of the concept of interest
- The theory which explains it
- The nature of any differences between the source and target cultures

This analysis can have three possible outcomes.

First, the researcher may conclude that there is no theoretical or logical reason why the construct should differ from the source culture to the target culture. If this is the case, we suggest that he or she then develop and test a draft target language instrument using ideas from Chapter 3 of this book.

Second, he or she may tentatively conclude that the construct is *emic*—unique to the source culture. Green and White (1976), for example, point out that cognitive consistency theories assume that people do not voluntarily hold discrepant attitudes. They argue that these theories are culturally bound and the concept of cognitive consistency has no equivalent in many cultures (p. 82). Such a conclusion may effectively terminate the line of research at hand.

Third, the researcher may tentatively conclude that the construct has both *etic* and *emic* components. Brislin (1993) argues that most important constructs are neither unique to one culture nor strictly universal. Rather, he holds, complex concepts are "often combinations of a common *etic* core plus culture-specific *emics*" (p. 74). Concepts of intelligence provide a good example of such an *etic/emic* mix. While most cultures accept the basic idea of differences in mental abilities, the concept manifests itself in different ways in different cultures. The Chi-Chewa of Zambia include a social responsibility factor in their concept of intelligence (Serpell, 1982). In many Western cultures, intelligence implies quick, accurate responses to problems. But among the Baganda people of Uganda (Wober, 1974) and in many Eastern cultures, intelligence is associated with slow, careful analysis. If logical support for such an *etic/emic* mix emerges, the researcher should describe the *emic* dimensions and how they relate to the *etic* dimensions. These dimensions should be reflected in the item pool used to develop the target language scales and eventually in the scale itself.

Empirical Tests of Conceptual Equivalence

Tests of the Similarity of Factorial Structures

An *etic* construct should have the same components (dimensions or internal structure) in the source and target cultures, by definition. Also, the relations among those components should be the same. If a measure captures the construct, the dimensions or internal structure should be the same in both cultures as well. Exploratory and confirmatory factor analysis are useful for determining if this is in fact the case. The former is normally used when creating a new measure, the latter when translating an existing instrument with a known factorial structure.

Farh, Lin, and Earley's (1997) work on organizational citizenship behaviors (OCB) serves as a good example of how *etic* and *emic* dimensions of a construct can be identified through examination of factorial structures. Bateman and Organ (1983) define OCB as individual behavior that is discretionary, not directly or explicitly recognized by the formal reward system, and that in the aggregate promotes the effective functioning of the organization.

Rather than blindly translating existing OCB scales, Farh et al. carefully examined the relationship between the constructs in the two cultures. Responses from a group of Chinese workers to a request to name common discretionary behaviors were used to create an item pool. Responses to these items from another sample of Chinese workers were then factor analyzed. Five dimensions—altruism, civic virtue, conscientiousness, protecting company resources, and interpersonal harmony—emerged. The first three dimensions are *etic*; they parallel those identified by Organ (1988) and Morrison (1994) in the United States. The last two dimensions are *emic*; they were not found in the United States. At the same time, two OCB dimensions (courtesy and sportsmanship) found in the United States did not emerge from the Farh et al. data. Further analysis revealed that the OCB construct, as measured by the Chinese scale related to other constructs in its nomological network in the Chinese sample as in the United States.

Exploratory Factor Analysis. The use of exploratory factor analysis (EFA) to test for conceptual equivalence requires the comparison of factorial structures responses of comparable samples from the source and target cultures. Unfortunately, there are no established rules or statistical tests available to compare the results of two exploratory factor analyses. Thus whether the scales are equivalent or not is the researcher's call. Irvine and Carroll (1980) suggest some criteria that can guide that judgment, however. They hold that confidence can be placed in the supposition that the scales are measuring the same thing if:

- The numbers of factors extracted from the two versions are the same
- The same items load on each factor
- The same proportions of the total variance are accounted for by each factor
- The intercorrelations among the factors extracted do not differ significantly

Sekaran and Martin (1982) analyzed 21 scales tapping individual perceptions of organizational, job, and personality characteristics of 267 white-collar employees in the United States, and 307 of their counterparts in India using translated versions of the scales. Using criteria similar to those suggested by Irvine and Carroll, they found that the organizational measures were much more consistent across the two cultures than were the job and personality scales.

When Irvine and Carroll's (1980) conditions are not met, common practice calls for the deletion of items with low or inappropriate factor loadings. This should be done with care, however. Researchers must assure themselves that the problem stems from a semantic flaw in the item, not from a lack of conceptual equivalence of the constructs. They must also check carefully to assure that sampling adequacy remains high. That is, that all aspects of the construct are represented in the target language version of the scale.

Confirmatory Factor Analysis. If the factorial structure of a scale has been established in one culture, confirmatory factor analysis (CFA) can be used to determine if the same factorial structure is present in a translated version of the scale. If the factorial structure of the original version of the scale is called the hypothesized model (M_h), some confidence can be placed in the supposition that the two versions of the scales are conceptually equivalent if:

- M_h fits the data better than the null model (i.e., one in which all items are totally unrelated)

- M_h fits the data better than the one-factor model (i.e., all items load on one single factor) when the original scale is a multidimensional one

- The general fit of M_h on the target language version is within the conventional acceptance limits

Usually, a difference in a chi-square test is employed to determine if the hypothesized model fits better than the null model and the one-factor model. In CFA, a chi-square statistic is associated with each and every model used to fit to the observed data. The smaller the model chi-square, the better is the fit between the observed data M_h. If the difference in two model chi-squares, which is also a chi-square distribution, is significant, the model with a smaller chi-square statistic fits the data better than the one with a larger chi-square. It should be noted that the chi-square difference test can only be applied on two models that are nested within one another. For a good introduction to confirmatory and exploratory factor analysis and the concept of nested models, readers are referred to Loehlin's (1992) excellent introduction to structural equation modeling.

A set of model goodness-of-fit indices is usually used to determine if the data collected in the second culture fit well into the hypothesized model. Some common model fit indices are the goodness-of-fit index (GFI) (Jöreskog & Sörbom, 1993), the comparative fit index (CFI) (Bentler, 1990), the Tucker-Lewis index (TFI) (Tucker & Lewis, 1973), the parsimony normed fit index (PNFI) (James, Mulaik, & Brett, 1982) and the root mean square error of approximation (RMSEA) (Steiger, 1990). Readers are referred to Jöreskog and Sörbom (1993) and Tanaka (1993) for good introductory discussions of various fit indices for confirmatory factor analyses.

Shek (1993) used CFA to compare the structures of two measures of well-being: the original General Health Questionnaire (GHQ) (Goldberg, 1972), which was developed in the United States, and its counterpart, the Chinese General Health Questionnaire (CGHQ). Based on the factorial structure of the GHQ, he hypothesized a five-factor model for the Chinese data: anxiety (nine items), depression (five items), inadequate coping (eight items), interpersonal dysfunctioning (six items), and sleep disturbances (two items). Factor analysis of the responses of 2150 secondary school students in Hong Kong showed that the hypothesized five-factor model fits the observed data well.

In another case, CFA indicated that the factorial structure of a scale differed from one culture to another. Hattie and Watkins (1981) examined the factorial structure of the Study Process Questionnaire (SPQ), which is used to measure the learning process in samples of 255 Australian and 173 Filipino university students. The original instrument operationalized three factors: utilizing, internalizing, and achieving. This three-factor structure was only replicated in the Australian sample. In the Filipino sample, a two-factor model fitted the data better than the three-factor model.

Tests of the Similarity of Positions in Nomological Nets

A researcher may also test for conceptual equivalence by examining the relationships of scale scores to other variables in its nomological network. The logic behind this argument is simple. One would expect that a relationship between two constructs found in one culture would occur in similar form in another. If, when one examines scores obtained with the target language measure, one finds substantial differences in the relationship between two constructs without any theoretical or logical justification, one must question the quality of the scale translation or the equivalence of the constructs.

Tests of the Similarity of Scores

Tests of conceptual equivalence discussed thus far require only that two versions of a scale measure the same construct with the same dimensions in two different cultures or that any differences are theoretically justifiable. They do not tell us whether a person in Germany who scores 5.3 on a measure of satisfaction with a visit to a theme park, for example, is as satisfied as one in France who scores the same in a French version of the same scale. Almost all examinations of similarity of scores use significance testing to determine whether the statistical properties of two versions of a scale differ, although different scholars focus on different types of statistical properties. Hui and Triandis (1983) identify three forms of score similarity:

- **Metric equivalence** exists when the properties of the two versions, such as item factor loadings, are the same or similar.
- **Scalar equivalence** means scores are directly comparable, i.e., 3.8 on, say, the Hindi version of a scale is equal to 3.8 on a Korean version.

- **Item equivalence** exists when individual item characteristics curves are similar across the two cultures.

We discuss the use of CFA and item response theory (IRT) as ways of testing for metric, scalar, and item equivalence in the following sections.

Confirmatory Factor Analysis. As discussed before, two versions of a scale are considered to be conceptually equivalent if they exhibit a general similarity in factorial structure or any differences are theoretically or logically justifiable. Usually this means the same number of factors (dimensions) emerge and the same items load on the same factors in an exploratory or a confirmatory factor analysis. Some scholars impose more stringent requirements, however.

For example, it is often argued that a necessary and sufficient condition to compare the means of two versions of a scale (in our case, two versions of the scale in different languages responded to by individuals in different cultures) is that the factor loadings of various items on their respective factors are the same across cultures (Bollen, 1989). Statisticians call this "factorial invariance" (Drasgow, 1984; Drasgow & Kanfer, 1985). On top of factorial invariance, Jöreskog and Sörbom (1989) call for tests of the equivalence of the variance-covariance matrices of the error terms as well. Only when all these parameters are the same can one compare the mean difference in scale scores between the two samples.

CFA is the most common technique used to test the equivalence of these scale parameters across cultures. Jöreskog and Sörbom (1993) provide detailed discussions of how this can be done using the CFA multisample procedure. The parameters of interest (e.g., factor loadings, error variances, and correlations of latent variables) are estimated using the multisample procedure while allowing the parameter estimates to be different between the two samples (Model 1 with model chi-square statistics χ_1^2). These parameters are then constrained to be the same in the two samples and a second set of estimates is obtained (Model 2 with model chi-square statistics χ_2^2). With constrained parameters, Model 2 must be nested within Model 1. The change in model chi-square between the two models (again, also a chi-square statistic) can be used as a test of the statistical significance of the constraint. If the change in model chi-square statistics is not significant, one concludes that the constrained parameters are the same in the two groups.

Item Response Theory. IRT (Lord, 1980; Hulin, Drasgow, & Parsons, 1983) has also been used to test for equivalence of measurement instruments. We do not have room to discuss IRT in detail. The following provides only a quick introduction to things you need to understand to apply it when testing for cultural equivalence. Ellis, Minsel, and Becker (1989) provide a more extensive discussion of how IRT can be used to test scale translations. Readers are referred to Lord (1980) or to Hambleton and Swaminathan (1985) for a general overview of IRT.

When used to test the conceptual equivalence of two versions of a measurement scale, IRT specifies a relationship between the subjects' observable scores on a scale and the unobservable traits assumed to underlie the scale. The most important output of an IRT is the item characteristic curve (ICC), a plot of the relationship between responses to an item and the latent construct hypothesized to underlie them. It represents graphically the probabilities of responding to an item in a certain specified manner at different levels of the latent construct (Hui & Triandis, 1985).

In ability testing, for example, the ICC of an item represents the probability of answering the item correctly given different levels of the respondent's ability. Most ICCs are S-shaped. Given a theoretical model of the ICC, IRT helps us estimate the parameters of the ICC for each item. A hypothetical ICC is shown in Exhibit 4.1.

The ICC shows that as the characteristic of the subject (e.g., ability) becomes higher, the chance of answering the item correctly increases. In Exhibit 4.1, a respondent with mean score ($\theta = 0$) on the latent trait would have a 50 percent chance, $p(\theta) = .5$, of answering the item correctly. The location of the point of inflection along the θ-axis (i.e., the point a on Exhibit 4.1) represents the difficulty of the item. If the whole ICC curve shifts to the right, a respondent needs to have a higher than average θ in order to have a .5 chance of answering the item correctly. The slope of the ICC at the point of inflection (i.e., the slope of the ICC at point b on Exhibit 4.1) informs us about the power of the item to distinguish individuals who are high in θ from those who are low in θ. If the slope is steep, only the high θ respondents answer the item correctly. In the extreme case that the slope is zero, i.e., a horizontal line, both high θ and low θ respondents have exactly the

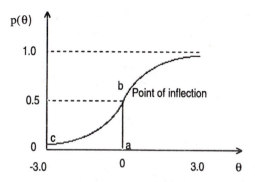

EXHIBIT 4.1. A hypothetical item characteristics curve.

same chance of answering the item correctly. The lower asymptote of the ICC along the y-axis (i.e., the point c on Exhibit 4.1) tells us the chance of answering the item correctly when the subject has the lowest θ score. It is therefore called the *pseudo-guessing parameter*— the chance of answering correctly irrespective of the subject's trait level.

Many models of ICC have been proposed. They differ in their mathematical modeling of the form of the ICC curve. However, the two-parameter model and the three-parameter model (Birnbaum, 1968) seem to be useful in a wide variety of situations. Candell and Hulin (1987) comment that:

> both the three-parameter and two-parameter logistic models have been shown to provide accurate approximations to item response data in content domains ranging from traditional multiple choice ability measures such as the SAT to measures of job satisfaction (p. 421).

In the three-parameter model, the ICC or the probability of a positive response to the ith item (e.g., answering "yes" to a dichotomous item) among subjects with attitude θ (i.e., a certain true score on the latent trait the scale purports to measure) is given as:

$$P_i(\theta) = c_i + (1 - c_i)\frac{1}{\{1 + e^{-Da_i(\theta - b_i)}\}}$$

where a is the discrimination parameter and is proportional to the slope of the ICC at its point of inflection, b is the difficulty parameter and the θ value that corresponds to $p(\theta) = .5$, c is the pseudo-guessing parameter that serves as an index of response acquiescence, D is a scaling constant usually set to 1.702 so that the ICC approximates a normal ogive curve, and the subscript i means that these parameters are estimated for the ith item in the scale. Candell and Hulin (1987) argue that:

> Equivalent item translations are different linguistic versions of the same items that evoke the specified response with the same probability among individuals with equal amounts of the trait. Two individuals who speak different languages but who have the same amount of the underlying trait should respond correctly or positively with equal probability to an item and its equivalent translation. (p. 420)

In IRT, an item is said to have differential item functioning (DIF) [lack metric equivalence in Hui & Triandis's (1983) lexicon] when the ICCs for the same items on the two versions of the scale differ by more than sampling error. DIF can be tested statistically with many different methods. Some commonly used methods are the parameter equating method, the Mantel-Haenszel method, and the model comparison method.

The parameter equating method (Lord, 1980): This method is the most widely used approach to testing DIF. It generates a chi-square statistic, which tests the differences between the two cultures' item parameters once they have been transformed to the same metric. Stocking and Lord (1983) derived a procedure for scale equating or the transformation of the item parameter estimates in one metric to those of another metric. This procedure "equates the item parameters from the two different samples to minimize the differences between θ estimates obtained by applying two sets of item parameters, estimated in two different samples, to a set of item responses" (Hulin & Mayer, 1986, p. 87).

The Mantel-Haenszel method. According to Huang, Church, & Katigbak (1997), the Mantel-Haenszel method may be the most common alternative to the parameter equating methods. In the Mantel-Haenszel method (Holland & Thayer, 1988; Mantel & Haenszel, 1959), a chi-square statistic is generated to test whether the actual frequencies of specific responses for one cultural group across various trait levels differ significantly from the frequencies that would be expected if there were no differences in the odds of a specific response for the two cultural groups.

The model comparison method (Camilli & Shepard, 1994; Thissen, Steinberg, & Wainer, 1993): This method of testing DIF is analogous to the test of factorial invariance in a confirmatory factor analysis. The item parameter (e.g., a, b, and c in a three-parameter model) for each item in the scale is first estimated using the combined sample from two cultures. This forms the compact model for the whole scale with one chi-square statistic as the measure of model fit (χ_1^2). While keeping the parameter estimates of all other items in the scale fixed, the a and b parameters of one specific item are then allowed to differ across the two samples. This generates another model with a different chi-square statistic (χ_2^2). The difference in the two model chi-square statistics provides a test of whether the a and b parameters for this particular item are the same across the two samples (Camilli & Shepard, 1994). It should be noted that even for the three-parameter model, only a and b are allowed to vary because Lord (1980) reasoned that the c parameter represents the probability of a correct response by individuals with infinitely low ability. Because it is unlikely that individuals of such low ability are actually present in the sample, any reasonable estimate of c will be able to fit the data about as well as any other (p. 186). As a result, Lord recommends estimating c by using both samples combined.

Hulin and Mayer (1986) provide a good example of the application of IRT in their test of a translated version of the Job Descriptive Index (JDI) (Smith, Kendall, & Hulin, 1969). They applied the two-parameter IRT model to estimate item parameters of the JDI using 500 Americans for the original English version and 308 Israeli upper-level workers for a Hebrew version. The Lord (1980) method and the Stocking and Lord (1983) scale equating method were used. They concluded that 45 of the 66 items were actually equivalent in the English and Hebrew versions.

Detailed information on procedures and examples of how they can be applied can be obtained from Ellis (1989); Huang, Church, and Katigbak (1997); Hulin, Drasgow, and Komocar (1982); and Smith, Tisak, Bauman, and Green (1991).

5. SOLVING NORMATIVE PROBLEMS

Each society has its own set of norms or conventions that influence individual behaviors. Normative problems for cross-cultural researchers exist when one or more of three kinds of conventions differ from the source to the target society:

- The openness with which particular topics are discussed
- The manner in which ideas are expressed
- The way in which strangers, particularly strangers asking questions, are treated

We explain each of these in the following paragraphs. We also examine six steps the researcher can take to reduce the impact of normative problems, recognizing at the same time that fully eliminating normative problems may prove to be a practical impossibility in some cases.

Kinds of Normative Problems

Openness With Which Topics Are Discussed

Societies differ substantially in the degree to which particular topics are discussed outside a small circle of intimates. Two are most likely to be critical from the perspective of the researcher. They are political opinions and facts about "personal matters": information about self and family.

Political Opinions. A society's political climate influences responses of those answering questionnaires. Respondents in societies where deviation from political orthodoxy is punished rightly worry more about the consequences of expressing political opinions than do respondents in societies in which free speech is protected.

Many of today's citizens of the People's Republic of China (PRC) lived through the Cultural Revolution when evidence of capitalistic inclinations led to public condemnation and when almost anyone—even a close family member—might denounce you. This experience made many Chinese extremely cautious about expressing political positions publicly and led to a general pattern of disguising attitudes and feelings. The researcher is especially likely to encounter this cautiousness when soliciting information from people who do not know her or him well.

In one case, although respondents were assured of anonymity, the mere presence of a numeric code on the cover page of a questionnaire triggered suspicion among a group of PRC citizens. Many individuals refused to participate in the study until they were reassured by the researcher about the uses to which the data were to be put and the consequences of answering in various ways. As a result, roughly double the time set aside for each administration in Hong Kong and Taiwan had to be allocated to each one in the PRC. Also, missing data among responses to politically sensitive questions was a greater problem in the PRC.

Information About Family and Personal Matters. Society-to-society differences also exist in the willingness of individuals to reveal information about themselves and their families. Inquiries about one's health, age, and family may be considered courteous expressions of sincere interest in some countries. The same queries are likely to be seen as "prying" in others.

Manner in Which Ideas Are Expressed

Societies differ not only in the degree to which open discussion of various topics is acceptable, but in the manner in which individuals express ideas and opinions as well. We identify six of these differences in the following paragraphs.

Self-Enhancement Versus Modesty. Societies vary in the degree to which individuals are expected to accentuate or downplay their accomplishments and capabilities. Hui and Triandis (1989) suggest that, in contrast to many Western societies where at least limited self-enhancement is expected, most Asian societies have strong modesty norms. This may stem from Confucian teachings that assign personal merit to those who are modest and self-disciplined.

Data from a sample of 982 leader-subordinate dyads in nine different organizations in Taiwan support this argument. Farh, Dobbins, and Cheng (1991) found that Taiwanese employees consistently rated their job performance lower than their supervisors rated that performance. This modesty occurred relatively uniformly across gender, educational level, and age groups.

Conformity Versus Assertiveness. Conformity refers to the tendency of respondents to answer in socially approved ways, especially if they believe that answers will be known by those holding positions of power. Assertiveness, on the other hand, is the tendency to freely express one's own opinions regardless of whether they conflict with the prevailing wisdom or with the positions of powerful individuals in the society.

Although conformity and its sibling social desirability are generally treated as individual-to-individual difference variables, considerable society-to-society differences also exist. Singaporeans, for example, generally trust the paternalistic styles of their leaders. They are not encouraged to develop and express independent judgments on many matters. This is in marked contrast to, say, Australians, who are much less likely to conform. Greenfield (1997) points out an extreme example of conformity among Mayan girls in rural Mexico:

> The notion that a girl would have an independent viewpoint, an independent piece of knowledge, or an independent perspective was not within their world view. Instead, they expected more knowledgeable mothers to answer for young girls and for members of the family grouping to answer cooperatively (p. 1118).

Directness Versus Indirectness. Directness refers to the tendency to answer questions clearly and unambiguously. Indirectness refers to the inclination to answer in ways that disguise or soften the answers. Kim and Paulk (1994) interviewed a group of Japanese and American managers. Nine of the twelve American managers commented on what they saw as a common tendency of the Japanese managers toward ambiguity and indirection, as opposed to the American tendency toward explicit and straightforward verbal and nonverbal expression.

Positional. Lonner (1990) uses the term "positional" to refer to differences in the degree to which respondents use extremes in rating scales, something that others sometimes discuss under the heading "central tendency." Gibbons, Hamby, and Dennis (1997) summarize the results of several studies of the degree to which various groups are likely to use extremes in responding to questionnaires. They conclude that:

- African Americans and Hispanic Americans are more likely to use the poles of scales than are non-Hispanic, white Americans.
- Greeks are more likely to use extremes than Americans. Chinese and Japanese are less likely to do so.

- The use of extremes is associated with high levels of individualism in a society.

Hui and Triandis (1989) offer two possible explanations of society-to-society differences in the use of extreme responses. First, they suggest, as indicated above, that it may reflect the level of individualism in the society. Second, they explore the possibility that when a society offers a richer vocabulary to describe degrees of agreement with an item, respondents have a higher chance of using the extreme anchors of the scale. Logically this makes sense. A rich vocabulary allows individuals to make precise distinctions among various levels of subjective judgment. When they are able to make such distinctions in their judgments, they may be more likely to use the anchors that match their judgments, extreme or not.

It is also possible that respondents in strongly paternalistic or high power distances societies (Hofstede, 1993) may not be accustomed to expressing their ideas and judgments freely and openly.

Ways in Which Stragers Are Treated

Different societies treat strangers, especially strangers asking questions, in different fashions. Pareek and Rao (1980) identify three norms governing responses to strangers. We consider them here.

Reticence. Reticence refers to the tendency of individuals to express ideas and opinions only to those they know well. Greenfield (1997) points out that strong reticence norms create a dilemma for the researcher. On the one hand, good practice in social science research normally calls for an impersonal relationship between researcher and respondent. On the other hand, obtaining more than the most superficial information from individuals in societies with strong reticence norms requires cultivating a close relationship. Greenfield (1997) points out three cases in which the researcher should expect to encounter reticence:

- In many societies, children are used to taking direction rather than to expressing opinions. They may be unwilling to answer questions themselves, turning instead to their elders whom they expect to answer in their place.
- In some societies questions are asked only to elicit needed information. The common research practice of using several similar questions

to increase the reliability of answers may generate irritation and anger (e.g., "I have already told you that! Why do you ask me again?") in such societies.

- In some societies, discussions of particular topics take place only in context. Attempts to ask questions about, say, child-rearing practices when food preparation is going on are unlikely to generate meaningful responses.

The Hospitality Norm. Many societies have traditions of hospitality in greeting strangers. Such a norm can be a two-edged sword for the researcher. On the one hand, individuals are likely to cooperate willingly in answering researchers' questions. Pareek and Rao (1980) indicate that this is especially likely to be true if the questions are seen as having little relevance to respondents' immediate problems and lives. On the other hand, the answers respondents give in such societies may be ones that they believe will please the researcher, not their own beliefs or opinions.

The Mischief Norm. Some societies see strangers as fair game. Individuals in such societies may take considerable pleasure in leading the naïve researcher astray. Pareek and Rao (1980) refer to this process as "game playing" and Brislin, Lonner, and Thorndike (1973) label it more bluntly "the sucker factor." Pareek and Rao indicate that in rural India such behavior is most commonly directed toward members of the opposite sex or those seen as threatening (e.g., tax collectors). Even Margaret Mead, one of the foremost anthropologists of the twentieth century, has been accused of falling victim to joking informants who convinced her that sexual promiscuity was the norm in Samoa when in fact the society was, by some standards, puritanical (Freeman, 1999).

Solutions to Normative Problems

The complexity and subtlety of normative problems make it difficult to present a comprehensive, step-by-step program for dealing with them. Thus the following paragraphs contain a grab bag of possible remedies from which researchers may choose those that best fit their situation.

Develop Close Relations With Respondents or
Use Trusted Agents

A common thread runs through much of the discussion of the sources of normative problems. Most of them would disappear if the researcher were an intimate of the respondent. Slomezynski (1969) demonstrated this fact in a study in which he held private discussions with friends who had previously been interviewed by a professional. He found that the publicly expressed opinions were much closer to governmental positions than those expressed to him.

Yet developing close relationships with respondents is not without problems. First, as Greenfield (1997) points out, good practice in social and behavioral research normally calls for an impersonal relationship between researcher and respondent. Second, time and cost constraints may make it impossible for the researcher to do so.

There is another alternative. The researcher may be able to tap into existing networks of close relationships. Though it yields a convenience sample rather than a randomly chosen one, this "friend-of-a-friend" approach may provide a practical substitute for developing relationships on one's own. For example, the second author was interested in obtaining information on unfair treatment in the workplace in the PRC. Rather than going directly to potential respondents, he asked each one of a group of his students in the PRC to obtain examples of unfair treatment from two friends or relatives. The procedure yielded a rich variety of incidents; one that he believes would not have emerged if he—a stranger—had approached the respondents directly.

Provide Assurances of Anonymity or Confidentiality

While assuring respondents of anonymity or confidentiality would seem to be a logical way of dealing with strong reticence norms, we frankly question the value of doing so if the topic is sensitive. Certain steps can be taken, however, that may make individuals more willing to respond openly:

- Names, demographic data, or affiliations that could be used to identify individuals should be requested only if absolutely necessary. Explain the reason for asking for the information, if it must be obtained, and spell out the steps that will be taken to safeguard the respondent's confidentiality.

- Questionnaires should not be numbered nor should they bear any other marks that might lead individuals to believe, correctly or incorrectly, that a specific instrument can be identified as theirs.
- Questionnaires should be returned to someone the respondents trust, rather than to someone unknown.
- Questions on sensitive topics should be asked only if absolutely necessary. If they must be included, they should be framed in as nonthreatening a manner as possible.

Rethink the Translator's Role

Unless one of the primary investigators takes on the job, researchers usually recruit what we call "translators of opportunity": individuals chosen with little concern for anything but the fact that they are (a) bilingual and (b) available. Further, once enlisted, too often the translator is treated as a low-level technician performing a mechanical procedure—a person whose only responsibility is to minimize semantic problems.

We second the position taken by Geisinger (1994), Sanders (1994), and Temple (1997), who believe that translators should be selected as much for their rich knowledge of the target society and culture as for their language facility. It is not too much of an exaggeration to say that fluency in the source and target languages is the least important asset that the translator should bring to the project.

Also, we believe that translators should be assigned far more important roles as members of research teams. They should contribute in major ways to understanding and solving conceptual and normative problems as well as semantic ones.

Use Decentering or Multicultural Teams

Collaboration among researchers in different cultures also can reduce normative problems (Douglas & Craig, 1983). Researchers from source and target cultures can examine the project and instruments and highlight possible normative problems. Carrying this idea a step further leads to endorsement of two techniques discussed in depth in Chapter 3—decentering and multicultural teams—as a way of minimizing normative problems as well as conceptual problems.

Decentering refers to a translation process in which the source and the target language versions are equally open to modification during the development phase (Brislin et al., 1973, pp. 37–38). The source language version need not be translated without change into the target language. In other words, the researcher does not focus on one of the languages. The multicultural team approach to item development avoids the whole issue of translation. It does so by creating functionally equivalent versions of the instrument in the target and source language or languages at the same time, rather than creating the source language version first and then deriving the target language version or versions from it. The researcher begins with a construct assumed to exist in both source and target societies and uses natives of the source and target societies to develop items unique to their own society in their own language.

Pilot Test and Field Test

Geisinger (1994) recommended a ten-step procedure for translation, which we discussed in Chapter 3. Steps four and five, pilot test the instrument and field test the instrument, can be used to determine, to a degree at least, the nature of normative problems in responses to translated scales.

Guthery and Lowe's (1992) random probe technique is particularly useful in teasing out potential normative problems during such tests. The random probe technique calls for a systematic program in which respondents are asked to explain what they think selected items mean. When the respondents verbalize their interpretation of the scale items, the researchers have a chance to understand respondents' frames of reference and possible concerns.

Check Statistically

Once pilot and field test data have been gathered, statistical tools can be used to check for normative problems. Statistical techniques such as simple t-tests and confirmatory factor analyses (CFAs) can be used to ensure that item means and variances do not differ significantly from one version of a scale to another. With similar item means and variances, researchers can be more confident that no normative problems exist.

For example, a simple t-test can be used as a preliminary check for the effects of a modesty norm. If the mean score of respondents in a society with a strong modesty bias is significantly lower on items calling for self-evaluation than that of a sample where such a norm is absent while the standard deviations are comparable, the researcher should be alert to the possibility that a modesty norm is at work. The major problem with this approach is that it is difficult for the researcher to tell whether any differences in mean scores stem from true society-to-society differences in latent variables or whether they reflect differences in norms governing answering questions.

To determine which of the two is at work, researchers may wish to determine whether the pattern appears at the construct level or item level. When the normative problem exists at the construct level, the pattern occurs for all items measuring a specific construct. For example, if self-ratings of political influence for Hong Kong citizens suffer from modesty biases, the same effect would be present when they are asked to evaluate their own political impact in different ways. However, if the problem only exists for individual items or operationalizations, an analysis of the statistical properties of each item will help to identify problem areas.

For example, when Curtis and Schmidt (1993) translated the Revised Behavior Problem Checklist (RBPRC) (Quay, 1983) into Spanish, they found that "passive, suggestible and easily led by others" (item 29) was not viewed as a negative characteristic by most of the Spanish-speaking respondents. As a result, that particular item did not perform its designed function even though it was linguistically well translated. If the normative problem exists at the item level instead of the construct level, a statistical analysis at the item level would identify possible problematic items that are affected by normative biases. Items that are affected by normative biases would have, for example, abnormally high or low mean scores, exceptionally larger or smaller item variances, and significantly different correlations with other items measuring the same construct.

CFA may be a useful way to identify some normative problems (e.g., the tendency to avoid extreme ratings). Although the problem of central tendency may not affect the mean scores of respondents in different societies, it could lead to a reduction in both the observed variances of each item and covariances among different items in the scale. With a large sample, those kinds of cross-cultural differences in response sets could be identified using CFA. Substantial differences in the observed variances and error variances of individual items while the mean scores are comparable would hint at a possible normative effect toward the center of the rating scale.

6. PUTTING IT ALL TOGETHER

What We Did in the Preceding Chapters

In the preceding chapters we laid out three sets of problems—semantic, conceptual, and normative—for the researcher and explained ways of dealing with them.

What We Do in This Chapter

In Chapter 6 we focus on practical guidance. Many of the ideas presented here are derived from previous chapters. Others, because they cut across problem boundaries or because they represent general approaches rather than specific steps, are discussed here for the first time.

The problems involved are far too complex to allow us to suggest many "cookbook" procedures. We can, however, suggest some rules of thumb that researchers can rely on as they attempt to deal with their unique circumstances. The discussion is organized around five key decisions that face the researcher:

- Should the researcher use self-report or non-self-report measures?
- Who should do the translating?
- Should the translator translate an existing instrument literally or adapt it?
- What rules of thumb should the translator follow in translating instructions, items, and response alternatives?
- How should the researcher test the target language instrument for equivalence?

The Questions

Should the Researcher Use Self-Report or Non-Self-Report Measures?

A point implicit in discussions in preceding chapters needs to be made explicitly here: The use of questionnaires and other self-report measures in non-Western, nonindustrialized cultures is a risky business. Ho (1988), for example, points to several reasons why Western research instruments may not work in Asia:

Certain formalized techniques—such as survey by questionnaire, interview or testing—are subject to severe restrictions in many Asian contexts on account of high illiteracy rates, apprehension in political matters, unfamiliarity with the role of and reluctance to serve as a research subject and so forth. (p. 57)

Despite numerous expressions of such concerns, substitutes for questionnaires and other self-report measures are rarely discussed in the literature of cross-cultural research. However, the researcher should carefully consider two other types of information-gathering methods before committing to the use of questionnaires and other self-report instruments.

One alternative to questionnaires and other self-report measures is outlined in Webb, Campbell, Schwartz, and Sechrest's classic *Unobtrusive Measures* (1966) and in Bochner's (1980) more focused discussion of the use of unobtrusive methods in cross-cultural research. Unobtrusive measures include:

- Examination of physical traces (e.g., a museum estimated interest in various exhibits by checking how frequently floor coverings had to be replaced in front of them).
- Various forms of structured observation, often of individuals who are unaware that they are being observed.
- Analysis of archival data (e.g., dissatisfaction with policing might be measured by counting numbers of formal complaints filed with citizen review boards).

Such methods can yield information but do not require direct questioning of respondents. Unobtrusive methods, with the exception of analysis of some forms of archival data, rule out semantic problems, by definition. Obviously, if no words are used, there can be no semantic problems.

The use of unobtrusive measures is not a cure-all, however. First, they do nothing to solve problems of conceptual and normative equivalence. Second, each one comes accompanied by its own set of problems. For example, the act of filing a formal complaint with the municipal government may represent an act of desperation in a high power distance society while it could be a relatively routine action in one where power distance is low.

Ho (1988) outlines a second alternative to Western-style interviews and questionnaires. He cites two examples of culturally appropriate questioning methods used by investigators in the Philippines. One researcher relied upon an adaptation of *pagtatanungtanong* (asking around), a Filipino pattern of interaction in which questions are asked only as they fit smoothly into an ongoing conversation. Another researcher studying homosexual prostitutes in Manila spent long periods cultivating a mode of interaction called *pakikisamaa* (being-along-with), before seeking to gather information, rather than relying on impersonal questionnaire or interview techniques.

Who Should Do the Translating?

In this section we consider the role the translator should play in the research team and his or her qualifications. An anonymous expert who reviewed this book in manuscript form suggested that the researcher should ideally be fluent in the source and target languages and do her or his own translating. We agree. However, as a practical matter, most researchers lack adequate knowledge of target languages. They must rely on others to translate their instruments.

The Translator's Role. Despite the translator's critical position in the process of creating equivalent measures, he or she is pretty much ignored in writings about cross-cultural data-gathering in the social and behavioral sciences. Frequently as well, the translator is treated as a technician performing a mechanical procedure—a person whose only responsibility is to minimize semantic problems. We believe that that translator should play a more important role as a member of the research team. Often the translator brings rich knowledge of the target culture and society to the table and can contribute in major ways to understanding and solving conceptual and normative problems as well as semantic ones (Temple, 1997).

The Translator's Qualifications. Geisinger (1994) challenges the near-universal practice of using what we refer to as "translators of opportunity"; individuals recruited with little concern for anything but the fact that they are bilingual and available. He argues that translators "must be fluent in both languages, extremely knowledgeable about both cultures, and expert in both the characteristics and the content measured on the instrument and the uses to which the . . . instrument will be put" (p. 306). Rarely will researchers find translators who meet all of Geisinger's criteria. Researchers normally must settle for a less-than-perfect mix of fluency, cultural awareness, and knowledge of the instrument and its uses. It is generally easier to teach a competent translator what he or she needs to know about the instrument and research program than it is to train someone in the target language and in the subtleties of the target culture. Thus, in our opinion, knowledge of the instrument and its uses should be the least important criterion for selecting translators in most cases.

Guthery and Lowe (1992) suggest that a native speaker of the target language, other things being equal, is a better translator than someone who learned it as a second language. They believe that a native speaker is more likely to be aware of nuances involved in expressing an idea in the target language. While this logic is seductive, research by de Groot, Dannenberg, and van Hell (1994) reveals only minor differences in patterns of factors influencing translations when bilingual individuals translated from their first language to their second and from their second to their first.

Guthery and Lowe (1992) argue further that those who acquired both languages by long immersion in the respective cultures deal with conceptual differences more effectively than those who learned the second language but were never immersed in the culture. Greenfield (1997) indirectly seconds this argument. She indicates that living on the margins of a culture at some point early in their lives is of great value to cross-cultural psychologists.

Should the Translator Translate Literally?

Literal translation of research instruments offers the promise of solving semantic problems, but offers nothing to those concerned about conceptual and cultural problems. Thus, in general, we recommend that the researcher adapt existing instruments rather than translating them word-by-word or phrase-by-phrase into the target language.

We qualify this recommendation in two ways. The first relates to the nature of the information the researcher is seeking. Questions asking for relatively simple factual information can frequently be translated directly. Those asking for more complex information—the bulk of the things in which social and behavioral scientists are interested—demand adaptation. The second deals with the kinship of the source and target languages. Where grammatical structures and word usage are similar, literal translation becomes easier. Thus a literal translation from French to Italian makes more sense than one from, say, Japanese to German.

What Procedures Should the Translator Use?

A Preliminary Caution. Before committing to a program of translation or adaptation, researchers should address an important issue. Cavusgil and Das (1997) point out that the existence of national cultures, i.e., homogeneous sets of values and beliefs coordinating with national boundaries, is an assumption, not a fact. They, building on the work of Cheng (1989), strongly recommend that the researcher take multiple samples within the target country in order to test for within-country differences. This is especially important in developing nations. Segall, Dasen, Berry, and Poortinga (1990, p. 63) point out that samples in developing countries often are biased toward urban, well-educated respondents, simply because their rural, poorly educated compatriots are inaccessible, making national generalizations risky if not impossible.

Translating Instructions. Relatively little has been written dealing specifically with the translation of instructions to accompany self-report research instruments. Irvine (1973), Irvine and Carroll (1980) and Segall et al. (1990) discuss some key issues involved in instructing what Irvine refers to as "test-alien" groups, however. While some of the recommendations in Irvine's (1973) piece are dated in the details and others are specific to ability testing, the three papers do provide the basis for seven useful recommendations:

1. The researcher should make every effort to assure that the research situation, which may seem strange, even frightening, to those unfamiliar with standard social science research procedures, is pleasant and non-threatening. In nations where ethnic, subcultural, or class differences are prominent, using administrators from the respondents' group may help put them at ease.

2. Target language instructions should not be literal translations of the source language instructions. They should relate to the experiences and sensibilities of the respondents.

3. Instructions should be given orally as well as in writing. Respondents should be provided with ample opportunities to ask questions and should be encouraged to do so.

4. The oral instructions should include detailed step-by-step illustrations. Researchers should make no assumptions regarding respondents' familiarity with the mechanics of the task they are being asked to perform.

5. Supervised practice should be provided.

6. If different individuals administer the instrument to different groups of respondents, care should be taken to assure that they follow the same methods and obtain equivalent results.

7. "Comprehension check" questions should be included to help the researcher identify respondents who, even after the instructions have been administered, do not understand the task they are being asked to perform. Segall *et al.* (1990) cite a study of optical illusions (Segall, Campbell, & Herskovits, 1963) in which four such questions were asked. One question showed the respondent a very short black line paired with a very long red one. The respondent was asked to indicate which of the two was longer. Failure to answer "red" alerted the researchers to the possibility that the respondent did not understand the instructions or the task.

Translating Items. Clearly the bulk of the preceding chapters deals with issues involved in translating items making up research instruments. We do not intend to repeat the material covered in earlier pages here. Rather we reemphasize only a few key ideas.

Brislin (1973) lists three item types that demand special attention from the translator:

1. Topics about which the respondent has no opinion and is thus unable to give a meaningful factual answer.

2. Topics that are especially sensitive to members of certain cultures.

3. Topics whose measurement demands greater sophistication in instrumentation. (p. 36)

Brislin's list provides an excellent beginning point, alerting the researcher to areas where difficulties are most likely to be encountered.

Dealing with item translation in general and with the problems Brislin identifies specifically is not easy, as explained in the earlier chapters. However, several things can help. First, the researcher should make every effort to create a pool of easily translatable items in the source language instrument or item pool. This should involve not only creating semantically translatable items, but those that are likely to transfer smoothly to the target society conceptually as well.

Second, Brislin (1973) suggests that the researcher aim to create multi-item scales containing a core of etic items supplemented by *emic* items appropriate for each target language and culture (p. 393). Tests of the relationship between the former and the latter provide an opportunity to increase confidence in the semantic and conceptual equivalence of the items.

Finally, Irvine (1973) (discussed in Irvine & Carroll [1980, pp. 462–463]) suggests that the researcher present items in order of ascending complexity. Doing so reduces the chance that respondents will misunderstand the items.

Translating Response Alternatives. Several researchers identify problems resulting from respondents' unfamiliarity with response formats and methods widely used in social and behavioral science research. Van de Viger and Leung (1997, p. 268) report an extreme case in which researchers administered the Porteus Maze Test, a paper-and-pencil test of intelligence, to respondents who had never before held a pencil. As one would expect, they performed poorly. They also point out that in some societies respondents may view the common social science practice of asking the same question several times in different forms as evidence of the researcher's stupidity (p. 315). Greenfield (1997) points out that some of her Mayan subjects understood a particular task well, but were thrown by the multiple-choice format. She argues that familiarity with it can be assumed only in cultures where formal Western-style education is the norm.

Paunonen and Ashton (1998) point out that the classic five or seven-point Likert-type item response format with *strongly disagree* and *strongly agree* as end-points is unfamiliar to respondents in many cultures (p. 153). Beyond that, they argue that responses from cultures where acquiescence is seen as a virtue may not mean the same thing as those from more assertive societies.

Unfortunately, none of the authors offers the researcher much concrete advice for solving the problems of translating response formats or for identifying those likely to be most useful in a given culture. Rather they advocate caution and cultural sensitivity in selecting response formats and suggest the need to pretest formats and to train respondents in their use.

How Should the Researcher Test for Equivalence?

The researcher should keep six things in mind as he or she goes about testing for equivalence.

Successful Back-Translation Is Not Proof of Equivalence. Translation/back-translation is the most commonly used method for determining the relationship of source and target language versions of an instrument. For example, Hwang, Yan, & Scherer's (1996) examination of 42 management studies published between 1989 and 1994 reveals the disturbing fact that the authors of 17 of them provided little meaningful information about the translation methods. Twenty-five of the remaining 29 used translation/back-translation, however.

Despite its popularity and the fact that it can be a useful tool for the development of target language instruments, **translation/back-translation *is not* an adequate test of the equivalence of the target and source language documents.** Three reasons underlie this conclusion.

The first and most compelling reason is that translation/back-translation deals only with semantic equivalence. It rarely tells us anything of importance about the conceptual or normative equivalence of the source and target language versions of the measure.

Second, back-translated versions of a source language document and the original may correspond with one another for the wrong reasons. Brislin (1970) suggests that translators sometimes share a set of rules for translating nonequivalent words or phrases. He points out, for example, that the Spanish *amigo* and the English *friend* are not always equivalent, but many translators ignore the subtleties and treat them as if they were. He also indicates that some translators may be able to make sense out of badly written target language documents and thus figure out the original source language wording, even if the target language version represents it poorly.

Third, the back-translated document may resemble the source language original even though the target language version may not convey the intended meaning to potential respondents. Because the initial translation may retain the grammatical structure of the source language or other clues, it may be easy to back-translate. However, it may appear strange, even nonsensical, to a monolingual target language speaker. Problems also may occur if the translator is aware that the document will be back-translated. He or she may focus on creating a target language document that is easy to convert back into the source language, even though it communicates key ideas poorly to the targeted respondents.

Whether a Given Construct Is Emic or Etic Is an Empirical Question. The degree to which key social science constructs are *emic* or *etic* is at the heart of the debate over conceptual equivalence. Positions on this issue range widely. The naïve and now largely abandoned assumption that North American social and behavioral science constructs and measures are universal stands at one extreme. At the other extreme is the equally unrealistic position that rejects all nonlocally developed constructs and measures.

We recommend a middle ground. We argue that the researcher is best served by treating the emic/etic nature of constructs and measures as something to be established empirically on a case-by-case basis.

Empirical Tests of Equivalence Should Be Driven by Theory. The limitations of existing empirical tests of equivalence combine with the complexity of the interactions among semantic, conceptual, and normative problems to make interpretation of the results of tests of equivalence problematic. The results tell the researcher that a problem exists, but not its source. Blind empiricism cannot answer the question: Does the lack of measured equivalence stem from (a) failure of the target language items to operationalize the variable in the same fashion as do items in the source language or (b) culture-to-culture differences in the relationships themselves or (c) society-to-society differences in behavioral norms?

A meaningful explanation of the results of tests of equivalence can occur only if it is theory-driven. Any effort to solve conceptual problems should begin with careful consideration of

- The constitutive definitions of the concept or construct of interest
- The theory behind it
- The nature of relevant differences between the source and target cultures

From this examination, the researcher develops hypotheses regarding emic and etic aspects of the construct and/or ways in which it manifests itself in the target language, culture, and society. These hypotheses guide the selection of tests of equivalence and the interpretation of their results.

Rigid Application of Statistical Tests of Equivalence Is Inappropriate.
We strongly endorse greater rigor in testing for equivalence of measurements in the social and behavioral sciences. At the same time, we
worry that researchers may rush to blind reliance upon confirmatory
factor analysis, item response theory, and the like, in judging equivalence. Given our current limited understanding of the practical implications of them as tests of equivalence across languages, cultures, and
societies and given the fact that major differences in factorial structures and item response curves often appear from sample to sample
within a single society, we recommend a relatively limited role for
these techniques. Certainly the tests should be performed where appropriate. Certainly the researcher should report the results. But we
believe that their use in a strict gate-keeping role is inappropriate.

Full Equivalence Is Not Always Needed. Tests of the equivalence of
scores are useful if the researcher wishes to aggregate scores from
the source and target versions in a single database or to compare
individual scores or distribution parameters (e.g., sample means) between the target language and culture and the source language and
culture. The researcher should decide whether tests of score equivalence are necessary by asking two simple questions. The first is, "Am
I interested in aggregating scores from the source and target societies in a single database?" The answer to this question is usually
"no." The second is, "How important is it to be able to compare individual scores or distribution parameters across source and target
samples?"

Certainly cases exist where an anthropologist is interested in finding
out, say, whether mean satisfaction is higher, the same, or lower in a
village in Thailand than it is among those living in a similar community
in Mexico. In such cases he or she needs to be assured that a score of
5.3 on the Thai version of the satisfaction scale means the same thing
as 5.3 on the Spanish version.

However, in our experience few researchers are interested in answering questions that have to do with the nature of relationships
between the source and target societies. Most are interested in answering questions about the similarity of relationships among variables *within* the source and target societies. For example, they may be
interested in knowing whether, as we pointed out in Chapter 4, the
Chinese language version of the General Health Questionnaire pre-

dicts academic performance of university students in China as it does in the United States.

Establishing Equivalence Is Not the Only Requirement. This book focuses on the establishment of equivalence of source and target language versions of research instruments. The establishment of equivalence is not the last step in the development of the target language instrument, however. As discussed in Chapter 2, the researcher must also determine and report the measured properties—most critically the reliability and validity—of the target language instrument. He or she cannot assume that the target language instrument's properties are the same as those of the source language version even though equivalence between the two has been established. Depending upon the uses to which it is to be put, he or she may also need to obtain and report evidence of the utility (cost-effectiveness) and legality of that instrument (Noe, Hollenbeck, Gearhart, & Wright, 1997). This is not always as large a task as it first might seem. Some of the procedures used to determine the construct equivalence of the source and target language instruments yield indications of the properties of the target language instrument as well.

A Concluding Note

In the preceding pages we provide some ideas that we believe can be of value to researchers confronted by the semantic, conceptual, and normative problems involved in translating questionnaires and other research instruments. We also recognize that in dissecting the problems and the solutions to them, something has inevitably been lost.

The missing piece has to do with the need for creative, sometimes radical, modifications and combinations of the techniques discussed in earlier chapters. For example, the researcher may find it desirable or even necessary to triangulate; to use cross-checks involving multiple forms of data-gathering (e.g., direct observation as a supplement to questionnaires and interviews) or multiple forms tests of their success in overcoming one or another type of problem.

NOTES

1. The Fyfe-Shaw system for categorizing things that can be measured in question-naires and other research instruments is not universally accepted. One question that has been raised with the authors of this book has to do with the reason why "percep-tions" is not listed separately. We believe that adding such a category would overlap with others already in Fyfe-Shaw's system (most importantly, attitudes and opinions).

2. "Decentering," which is also included in Guthery and Low's list, is treated in the following section.

3. Brislin writes of "passive words" in his 1980 work. We have chosen to follow the wording of the 1973 version in the belief that it is more easily understood.

REFERENCES

BARRICK, M. R., & MOUNT, M. K. (1991). The big five personality dimensions and job performance: A meta-analysis. *Personnel Psychology, 44*, 1–26.

BATEMAN, T. S., & ORGAN, D. W. (1983). Job satisfaction and the good soldier: The relationship between affect and employee citizenship. *Academy of Management Journal, 26*, 587–595.

BECKER, T. E., BILLINGS, D. M., EVELETH, D. M., & GILBERT, N. L. (1996). Foci and bases of employee commitment: Implications for job performance. *Academy of Management Journal, 39*, 464–482.

BEHLING, O., & McFILLEN, J. M. (1997). Translating questionnaires: Personal experiences and general conclusions. *Proceedings of the XIV Annual Pan-Pacific Conference* (pp. 10–12). Kuala Lumpur: Pan-Pacific Business Association.

BENTLER (1990). Comparative fit indexes in structural models. *Psychological Bulletin, 107*, 238–246.

BERRY, J. W. (1969). On cross-cultural comparability. *International Journal of Psychology, 4*, 119–128.

BIRNBAUM, A. (1968). Some latent trait models and their use in inferring an examinee's ability. In F. M. Lord & M. R. Novick (Eds.), *Statistical theories of mental test scores*. Reading, MA: Addison-Wesley.

BOCHNER, S. (1980). Unobtrusive measures in cross-cultural experimentation. In H. C. Triandis & J. W. Berry (Eds.), *Handbook of cross-cultural psychology* (Vol. 2, pp. 389–444). Boston: Allyn & Bacon.

BOLLEN, K. A. (1989). *Structural equations with latent variables*. New York: Wiley.

BRISLIN, R. (1970). Back-translation for cross-cultural research. *Journal of Cross-Cultural Psychology, 1*, 185–216.

BRISLIN, R. W. (1973). Questionnaire wording and translation. In R. W. Brislin, W. J. Lonner, & R. M. Thorndike (Eds.), *Cross-cultural research methods* (pp. 32–58). New York: John Wiley.

BRISLIN, R. W. (1980). Translation and content analysis of oral and written materials. In H. C. Triandis & J. W. Berry (Eds.), *Handbook of cross-cultural psychology* (Vol. 2, pp. 389–444). Boston: Allyn & Bacon.

BRISLIN, R. (1993). *Understanding culture's influence on behavior* (pp. 74–76). Fort Worth: Harcourt Brace College Publishers.

BRISLIN, R. W., Lonner, W. J., & Thorndike, R. M. (Eds.), (1973). *Cross-cultural research methods*. New York: John Wiley.

CAMILLI, G., & SHEPARD, L. A. (1994). *Methods for identifying biased test items*. Thousand Oaks, CA: Sage.

CANDELL, G. L., & HULIN, C. L. (1987). Cross-national and cross-cultural comparisons in scale translations—Independent sources of information about item nonequivalence. *Journal of Cross-Cultural Psychology, 17*, 417–460.

CAVUSGIL, S. T., & DAS, A. (1997). Methodological issues in empirical cross-cultural research: A survey of the management literature and a framework. *Management International Review, 37*, 71–96.

64

CHEN, Z. X. (1997). *Loyalty to supervisor, organizational commitment and employee outcomes: The Chinese case*. Unpublished doctoral thesis.

CHEUNG, C. K., & BAGLEY, C. (1998) Validating an American scale in Hong Kong: The center for epidemiological studies depression scale (CES-D). *Journal of Psychology, 132,* 169–186.

CHEUNG, J. L. C. (1989). Toward a contextual approach to cross-national organizational research: A macro perspective. *Advances in International Comparative Management, 4,* 3–18.

CROWNE, D. P., & MARLOW, D. (1964). *The approval motive.* New York: Wiley.

CURTIS, P. A., & SCHMIDT, L. L. (1993). A Spanish translation of the revised behavior problem checklist. *Child Welfare League of America, 72,* 453–460.

DAVIDSON, A. R., JACCARD, J. J., TRIANDIS, H. C., MORALES, M. L., & DIAZ-GUERRERO R. (1976). Cross-cultural model testing: Toward a solution of the etic-emic dilemma. *Intenational Journal of Psychology, 11,* 1–13.

DE GROOT, A. M. B., DANNENBERG, L., & VAN HELL, J. G. (1994). Forward and backward word tranlation by bilinguals. 600–629.

DEVELLIS, R. F. (1991). *Scale Development: Theory and Applications.* Newbury Park, CA: Sage.

DOUGLAS, S. P., & CRAIG, S. (1983). *International Marketing Research.* Englewood Cliffs, NJ: Prentice-Hall.

DRASGOW, F. (1984). Scrutinizing psychological tests: Measurement equivalence and equivalent relations with external variable are the central issues. *Psychological Bulletin, 95,* 134–135.

DRASGOW, F., & KANFER, R. (1985). Equivalence of psychological measurement in heterogeneous populations. *Journal of Applied Psychology, 70,* 662–680.

ELLIS, B. B. (1989). Differential item functioning: Implications for test translations. *Journal of Applied Psychology, 74,* 912–921.

ELLIS, B. B., MINSEL, B., & BECKER, P. (1989). Evaluation of attitude survey translations: An investigation using item response theory. *International Journal of Psychology, 24,* 665–684.

FARH, J., DOBBINS, G. H., & CHENG, B. (1991). Cultural relativity in action: A comparison of self-ratings made by Chinese and U. S. workers. *Personnel Psychology, 44,* 129–147.

FARH, J. L., LIN, S., & EARLEY, P. C. (1997). Impetus for action: A cultural analysis of justice and organizational citizenship behavior in Chinese society. *Administrative Science Quarterly, 42,* 421–444.

FREEMAN, D. (1999). *The fateful hoaxing of Margaret Mead.* Boulder CO: Westview Press.

FYFE-SCHAW, C. (1995) Questionnaire design. In G. M. Breakwell, S. Hammond, & C. Fife-Schaw (Eds.), *Research methods in psychology* (pp. 174–193). London: Sage.

GASQUOINE, P. G. (1997). American psychological imperialism in the fourth world. *American Psychologist, 52,* 570–571.

GEISINGER, K. F. (1994). Cross-cultural normative assessment: Translation and adaptation issues influencing the normative interpretation of assessment instruments. *Psychological Assessment, 6,* 304–312.

GEORGOPOULOS, B. S., & MANN, F. C. (1962). *The community general hospital.* New York: Macmillan.

65

GIBBONS, J. L., HAMBY, B. A., & DENNIS, W. D. (1997) Researching gender-role ideologies internationally and cross-culturally. *Psychology of Women Quarterly, 21,* 151–170.

GIELEN, U. P. (1982). A comparison of ideal self-ratings between American and German university students. In L. L. Adler (Ed.), *Cross-cultural research at issue* (pp. 275–288). New York: Academic Press.

GOLDBERG, D. P. (1972). *The detection of psychiatric illness by questionnaire.* Oxford: Oxford University Press.

GREEN, R. T., & WHITE, P. D. (1976). Methodological considerations in cross-national consumer research. *Journal of International Business Studies, 14,* 81–87.

GREENFIELD, P. M. (1997). You can't take it with you: Why ability assessments don't cross cultures. *American Psychologist, 52,* 1115–1124.

GUTHERY, D., & LOWE, B. A. (1992). Translation problems in international marketing research. *Journal of Language for International Business, 4,* 1–14.

GUTHRIE, G. M. (1961). *The Filipino child in Philippine society.* Manila: Philippine Normal College Press.

HAMBLETON, R. K. (1993). *Technical standards for translating test and establishing test score equivalence.* Symposium presented at the 101 Annual Convention of the American Psychological Association, Toronto, Ontario, Canada.

HAMBLETON, R. K., & SWAMINATHAN, H. (1985). *Item response theory—Principles and applications.* Boston: Kluwer-Nijhoff Publishing.

HATTIE, J. A., & WATKINS, D. (1981). Australian and Filipino investigations of the internal structure of Biggs' new Study Process Questionnarie. *British Journal of Educational Psychology, 51,* 241–244.

HEMPHILL, J. K. (1950). *The leader behavior description questionnaire.* Columbus, OH: Ohio State University Personnel Research Board.

HO, D. Y. F. (1988). Asian psychology: A dialogue on indigenization and beyond. In A. C. Paranjpe, D. Y. F. Ho, & R. W. Reiber (Eds.), *Asian contributions to psychology* (pp. 1–77). New York: Praeger.

HO, D. Y. F. (1998). Indigenous psychologies. *Journal of Cross-Cultural Psychology, 29,* 88–103

HOFSTEDE, G., & Bond, M. H. (1988). The Confucius connection: From cultural roots to economic growth. *Organizational Dynamics, 16,* 4–21.

HOFSTEDE, G. (1993). Cultural constraints in mangement theories. *Academy of Management Journal, 7,* 81–93.

HOLLAND, P. W., & THAYER, D. T. (1988). Differential item functioning and the Mantel-Haenszel procedure. In H. Wainer & H. I. Braun (Eds.), *Testing validity.* Hillsdale, NJ: Lawrence Erlbaum.

HOUSE, R. J., & RIZZO, J. R. (1972). Role conflict and ambiguity as critical variables in a model of organizational behavior. *Organizational Behavior and Human Performance, 7,* 465–505.

HUANG, C. D., CHURCH, A. T., & KATIGBAK, M. S. (1997). *Journal of Cross-Cultural Psychology, 28,* 192–218.

HUI, C. H., & TRIANDIS, H. C. (1983). Multistrategy approach to cross-cultural research—The case of locus of control. *Journal of Cross-Cultural Psychology, 14,* 65–83.

66

HUI, C. H., & TRIANDIS, H. C. (1985). Measurement in cross-cultural psychology—A review and comparison of strategies. *Journal of Cross-Cultural Psychology, 16,* 131–152.

HUI, C. H., & TRIANDIS, H. C. (1989). Effects of culture and response format on extreme response style. *Journal of Cross-Cultural Psychology, 20,* 296–309.

HULIN, C. L., DRASGOW, F., & KOMOCAR, J. (1982). Application of item response theory to analysis of attitude scale translations. *Journal of Applied Psychology, 67,* 818–825.

HULIN, C. L., DRASGOW, F., & PARSONS, C. K. (1983). *Item response theory: Applications to psychological measurement.* Homewood, IL: Irwin.

HULIN, C. L., & MAYER, L. J. (1986). Psychometric equivalence of a translation of the Job Descriptive Index into Hebrew. *Journal of Applied Psychology, 71,* 83–94.

HWANG, C., YAN, W., & SCHERER, R. H. (1996). Understanding managerial behaviors in different cultures: A review of instrument translation methodology. *International Journal of Management, 13,* 332–339.

IRVINE, S. H. (1973). Tests as inadvertent sources of discrimination in personnel decisions. In P. Watson (Ed.), *Psychology and race* (pp. 453–461). London, Penguin Books.

IRVINE, S. H., & CARROLL, W. K. (1980). Testing and assessment across cultures: Issus in methodology and theory. In H. C. Triandis & J. W. Berry (Eds.), *Handbook of cross-cultural psychology: methodology* (Vol. 2). Boston: Allyn & Bacon.

JAMES, L. R., MULAIK, S. A., & BRETT, J. M. (1982). *Causal analysis: Assumptions, models, and data.* Beverly Hills, CA: Sage.

JÖRESKOG, K. G., & SÖRBOM, D. (1989). *LISREL VII: A guide to the program and applications.* Chicago: SPSS.

JÖRESKOG, K., & SÖRBOM, D. (1993). *LISREL 8: Structural equation modeling with the SIMPLIS command language* (pp. 111–132). Chicago: Scientific Software International.

KALLEBERG, A. L., KNOKE, D., MARSDEN, P. V., & SPAETH, J. L. (1996). *Organizations in America.* Thousand Oaks, CA: Sage.

KELLEHEAR, A. (1993). *Unobtrusive research: A guide to methods.* Paul & Co. Publishers Consortium.

KIM, Y. Y., & PAULK, S. (1994). Intercultural challenges and personal adjustments: A qualitative analysis of the experiences of American and Japanese co-workers. In R. L. Wiseman & R. Shuter (Eds.), *Communicating in multinational organizations.* Thousand Oaks, CA: Sage.

LIKERT, R. (1961). *New patterns of management.* New York: McGraw-Hill.

LOEHLIN, J. C. (1992). *Latent variable models—An introduction to factor, path and structural analysis* (2nd ed.). Hillsdale, NJ: Lawrence Erlbaum.

LONNER, W. J., & IBRAHIM, F. A. (1996). Appraisal and assessment in cross-cultural counseling. In P. B. Pedersen, J. G. Draguns, W. J. Lonner, & J. E. Trimble (Eds.), *Counseling across cultures* (4th ed.). Newbury Park, CA: Sage.

LORD, F. M. (1980). *Applications of item response theory to practical testing problems.* Hillsdale, NJ: Lawrence Erlbaum.

MANTEL, N., & HAENSZEL, W. (1959). Statistical aspects of the analysis of data from retrospective studies of disease. *Journal of the National Cancer Institute, 22,* 719–748.

MERENDA, P. F. (1982). The Rhode Island Pupil Identification Scale (RIPIS) in cross-cultural perspective. In L. L. Adler (Ed.), *Cross-cultural research at issue* (pp. 125–143). New York: Academic Press.

MILLER, D. C. (1991). *Handbook of research design and social measurement* (5th ed.). Newbury Park, CA: Sage.

MITSUMI, J., & PETERSON, M. F. (1985). The performance-maintenance (PM) theory of leadership: Review of a Japanese research program. *Administrative Science Quarterly, 30,* 198–223.

MORRISON, E. W. (1994). Role definitions and organizational citizenship behavior: The importance of the employees' perspective. *Academy of Management Journal, 37,* 1543–1567.

NOE, R. A., HOLLENBECK, J. R., GEARHART, B., & WRIGHT, P. (1997). *Human resource management: Gaining a competitive advantage* (2nd ed.). New York: Irwin.

NOWAK, S. (1976). Meaning and measurement in comparative social studies. In *Understanding and prediction: Essays in the methodology of social and behavioral theories,* (pp. 104–132). Dordrecht, Holland: D. Reidel.

NUNNALLY, J. C. (1978). *Psychometric theory* (2nd ed.). New York: McGraw-Hill.

ORGAN, D. W. (1988). *Organizational citizenship behavior: The good soldier syndrome.* Lexington, MA: D. C. Heath.

PAREEK, U., & RAO, T. V. (1980). Cross-cultural surveys and interviewing. In H. C. Triandis & J. E. Berry (Eds.), *Handbook of cross-cultural psychology, Vol. 2: Methodology* (pp. 127–180). Boston: Allyn & Bacon.

PARRY, G., & WARR, P. B. (1980). The measurement of mothers' work attitudes. *Journal of Occupational Psychology, 53,* 245–252.

PAUNONEN, S. V., & ASHTON, M. C. (1998). The structured assessment of personality across cultures. *Journal of Cross-Cultural Psychology, 29,* 150–170.

PRICE, J. L. (1997). Handbook of organizational measurement. *Manpower, 18,* nos. 4–7.

QUAY, H. C. (1983). A dimensional approach to children's behavior disorder: The revised behavior problems checklist. *School Psychology Review, 12,* 244–249.

RUBENSTEIN, G. (1996). Two people in one land: A validation study of Altemeyer's right-wing authoritarianism scale in the Palestinian and Jewish societies in Israel. *Journal of Cross-Cultural Psychology, 27,* 216–230.

SAITO, S., NOMURA, N., NOGUCHI, Y., & TEZUKA, I. (1996). Translatability of family concepts into the Japanese culture: Using the Family Environment Scale. *Family Process, 35,* 239–257.

SALGADO, J. (1997). The five factor model and job performance in the European Community. *Journal of Applied Psychology, 82,* 30–43.

SANDERS, D. (1994). Methodological considerations in comparative cross-national research. *International Social Science Journal, 46,* 513–521.

SEAGALL, M. W. (1979). *Cross-cultural Psychology.* Monterey, CA: Wadsworth.

SEGALL, M. H., CAMPBELL, D. T., & HERSKOVITS, M. J. (1963). Cultural differences in the perception of geometric illusions. *Science, 138,* 769–771.

SEGALL, M. H., DASEN, P. R., BERRY, J. W., & POORTINGA, Y. H. (1990). *Human behavior in global perspective: An introduction to cross-cultural psychology.* New York: Pergamon Press.

68

SEKARAN, U., & MARTIN, H. J. (1982). An examination of the psychometric properties of some commonly researched individual differences, job and organizational variables in two cultures. *Journal of International Business Studies, 13*, 51–65.

SERPELL, R. (1982). Measures of perception, skills, and intelligence: The growth of a new perspective on children in a Third World country. In W. W. Hartup (Ed.), *Review of Child Development Research* (Vol. 6). Chicago: University of Chicago Press.

SHAVELSON, R. J., HUBNER, J. J., & STANTON, G. C. (1976). Self-concept: Validation of construct interpretations. *Review of Educational Research, 46*, 407–441.

SHEK, D. T. L. (1993). Factor structure of the Chinese version of the general health questionnaire (GHQ-30): A confirmatory factor analysis. *Journal of Clinical Psychology, 49*, 678–684.

SLOMEZYNSKI (1969). Conditions of interview: Their impact upon statements of respondents. *Polish Sociological Bulletin, 20*, 125–135.

SMITH, C. S., TISAK, J., BAUMAN, T., & GREEN E. (1991). Psychometric equivalence of a translated circadian rhythm questionnaire: Implications for between- and within-population assessments. *Journal of Applied Psychology, 76*, 628–636.

SMITH, P. C., KENDALL, L. M., & HULIN, C. L. (1969). *Measurement of satisfaction in work and retirement*. Chicago: Rand McNally.

STEIGER, J. H. (1990). Structural model evaluation and modification: An internal estimation approach. *Multivariate Behavioral Research, 25*, 173–180.

STOCKING, & LORD (1983). Developing a common metric in item response theory. *Applied Psychological Measurement, 7*, 201–210.

SUCHMAN, E. A. (1964). The comparative method in social research. *Rural Sociology, 29*, 123–137.

SUURMEIJER, T. P. B. M., DOEGLAS, D. M., BRIANCON, S., KRUNEN, W. P., BOUDIEN, K., SANDERMAN, R., MOUM, T., BJELLE, A., & VAN DEN HEUVEL, W. J. A. (1995). The measurement of social support in the European research on incapacitating diseases and social support: The development of the Social Support for Transactions questionnaire (SSQT). *Social Science and Medicine, 40*, 1221–1229.

TANAKA, J. S. (1993). Multifaceted conceptions of fit in structural equation models. In K. A. Bollen & J. S. Long (Eds.). *Testing structural equation models*. Newbury Park, CA: Sage.

TEMPLE, B. (1997). Watch your tongue: Issues in translation and cross-cultural research. *Sociology, 31*, 607–618.

THISSEN, D., STEINBERG, L., & WAINER, H. (1993). Detection of differential item functioning using the parameters of item response models. In P. W. Holland & H. Wainer (Eds.), *Differential item functioning: Theory and practice*. Hillsdale, NJ: Lawrence Erlbaum.

TUCKER, L. R., & LEWIS, C. (1973). The reliability coefficient for maximum likelihood factor analysis. *Psychometrika, 38*, 1–10.

VAN DE VIGER, F., & LEUNG, K. (1997). Methods and data-analysis in comparative research. In J. W. Berry, Y. H. Poortinga, & J. Pandey (Eds.), *Handbook of cross-cultural psychology, Vol. 1: Theory and method*. Boston: Allyn & Bacon.

WARR, P., COOK, J., & WALL, T. (1979). Scales for the measurement of some attitudes and aspects of psychological well-being. *Journal of Occupational Psychology, 52*, 129–148.

WEBB, E. J., CAMPBELL, D. T., SCHWARTZ, D. T., & SECHREST, L. (1966). *Unobtrusive measures: Nonreactive Research in the Social Sciences*. Chicago: Rand McNally.

WERNER, O., & CAMPBELL, D. T. (1970). Translating, working through interpreters, and problems of decentering. In R. Naroll & R. Cohen (Eds.), *A handbook of method in cultural anthropology* (pp. 398–420). New York: Columbia University Press.

WIERZBICKA, A. (1997). The double life of a bilingual. In M. H. Bond (Ed.), *Working at the interface of cultures: Eighteen lives in social science* (pp. 113–125). London: Routledge.

WOBER, M. (1974). Towards an understanding of the Kiganda concept of intelligence. In J. W. Berry & P. R. Dasen (Eds.), *Culture and cognition*. London: Methuen.

WOLLACK, S., GOODALE, J. G., WIJTING, J. P., & SMITH, P. C. (1971). Development of a survey of work values. *Journal of Applied Psychology, 55*, 331–338.

YANG, K. S. (1997). Indigenizing westernized Chinese psychology. In M. H. Bond (Ed.), *Working at the interface of cultures: Eighteen lives in social science* (pp. 62–76). London: Routledge.

ABOUT THE AUTHORS

ORLANDO BEHLING (Ph.D., University of Wisconsin, Madison) is Distinguished University Professor Emeritus at Bowling Green State University and a principal of Behling Associates. His primary research interests are in the area of employee selection, leadership and research methods.

KENNETH S. LAW (Ph.D., University of Iowa) is Associate Professor in the Department of Management at Hong Kong University of Science and Technology. His research focuses on human resource management, management in the People's Republic of China, and methodological issues in management research.